The 360 Degree Brand in Asia

in Asia

Creating more effective marketing communications

The 360 Degree Brand in Asia

Creating more effective marketing communications

by

Mark Blair
Richard Armstrong
Mike Murphy

John Wiley & Sons (Asia) Pte Ltd

Copyright © 2003 John Wiley & Sons (Asia) Pte Ltd
Published by John Wiley & Sons (Asia) Pte Ltd
2 Clementi Loop, #02-01, Singapore 129809

All rights reserved.

No part of this publication may be reproduced, stored in a retrieval system or transmitted in any form or by any means, electronic, mechanical, photocopying, recording, scanning or otherwise, except as expressly permitted by law, without either the prior written permission of the Publisher, or authorization through payment of the appropriate photocopy fee to the Copyright Clearance Center. Requests for permission should be addressed to the Publisher, John Wiley & Sons (Asia) Pte Ltd, 2 Clementi Loop, #02-01, Singapore 129809, tel: 65-6463-2400, fax: 65-6464-6912, e-mail: enquiry@wiley.com.sg.

This publication is designed to provide accurate and authoritative information in regard to the subject matter covered. It is sold with the understanding that the publisher is not engaged in rendering professional services. If professional advice or other expert assistance is required, the services of a competent professional person should be sought.

Other Wiley Editorial Offices

John Wiley & Sons, Inc., 111 River Street, Hoboken, NJ 07030, USA
John Wiley & Sons Ltd, The Atrium, Southern Gate, Chichester P019 8SQ, England
John Wiley & Sons (Canada) Ltd, 22 Worcester Road, Rexdale, Ontario
    M9W 1L1, Canada
John Wiley & Sons Australia Ltd, 33 Park Road (PO Box 1226), Milton, Queensland 4064,
    Australia
Wiley-VCH, Pappelallee 3, 69469 Weinheim, Germany

Library of Congress Cataloging-in-Publication Data:

0-470-82057-8

Typeset in 12/16 points, Cochin by Linographic Services Pte Ltd
Printed in Singapore by Saik Wah Press Pte Ltd
10 9 8 7 6 5 4 3 2

for:

Liam
Christopher
Jonathan
Daniel
Oliver
&
Finley

Contents

Interludes
Culturally Unique Media

Acknowledgments

The catalyst for this book was a rather grand-sounding speech we made called "360 Degree Branding: The New Mantra for Strategic Marketing Communications".

But the real idea for this book goes back way before us, to the many people in the Ogilvy & Mather Worldwide organization who, in one way or another, espoused the values of broad-based communication thinking. In fact, it goes back to David Ogilvy himself. Around the world, David's books, beautifully written and far superior to the words we have penned here, are often described as "advertising books". While they certainly include many advertising examples, David himself was anything but just an "ad man". His first love was direct marketing, something he called his secret weapon. And that was over 50 years ago!

This book goes back, too, to the Ogilvy team that developed the philosophy of 360 Degree Brand Stewardship[SM], which helped revive and refresh the Ogilvy brand itself, and to those who embraced and added to that philosophy, and made 360 Degree Brand Stewardship[SM] the very soul of Ogilvy around the world.

Today, the company is well placed to talk about this topic. Not only is Ogilvy one of the most successful advertising agencies worldwide, working with a host of international clients in most countries around the world, it is also one of the largest direct marketing networks, the world's largest interactive network (not just in size, but also clearly recognized as a world leader by industry peers and award shows worldwide) and one of the largest and most successful public relations networks worldwide. It is not without reason that it is known as the Ogilvy Group.

To the people in all of these businesses, and more not mentioned, we owe our thanks. So, too, do we owe a debt of gratitude to the thousands of people who practice 360 Degree brand thinking for their clients across the world on a daily basis, some of whom are represented in the case studies that follow. Finally, we owe our thanks to the many clients, particulary those mentioned in the following pages, for their support, and for allowing their brands to be included here.

There are several individuals who have helped in many ways to make this book a reality. We would like to thank David Mayo at RedCard for his enthusiasm and encouragement; Aki Hoshide in Tokyo and Jessica Lai in Singapore for their ever-helpful assistance; Andrew Samuel in Sri Lanka, Mike Cooper, John Goodman and Matthew Anderson in Hong Kong, and Indira Nair in Kuala Lumpur for their valuable contributions; Eleanor Mascheroni, Nora Slattery and Shelly Lazarus in New York for their support; and particularly Miles Young here in Asia for his sponsorship and guidance. Finally, a huge word of thanks to John Owen, Janis Soo and Nick Wallwork at John Wiley for their unfailing good humor, patience and persistence in seeing this project through.

Needless to say, any fuzzy thinking, faulty logic, poor grammar or just plain mistakes — blame us!

Preface

The Asia-Pacific region, from India and Pakistan in the West to Japan and South Korea in the East, is one which encompasses every type of consumer terrain: from emerging markets like Vietnam or Indonesia, to vast centers of turbo-growth like China, as well as first-world markets like Singapore, Japan and Hong Kong. It is without doubt the most exciting, dynamic and stimulating place on earth to be working in the marketing communications industry today.

For the in-comer, it is refreshing to be able to work within such a breadth and depth of diversity — of people, of brands and of consumer cultures. It is also invigorating to be propelled by the appetite for new and innovative marketing thinking and practices that Asia exhibits. "Brand culture" has taken secure root within both Asian and multinational corporations across the region, and the orientation programs about the benefits of branding, which characterized so much of our work in the mid '90s, have long since been relegated to the trash can. No other regional market can offer the variety or stimulation that Asia can.

For the vast talent pool of young, enthusiastic and passionate Asian employees working in marketing and brand communications (many of whom are "expatriates" themselves — the intra-Asian transfer network is prolific), it is no doubt reassuring to know that in many areas of the "brand business", they already lead the world in terms of new thinking, new ideas and new solutions. Certainly, within the Ogilvy & Mather global network, Asia-Pacific has not only embraced the concept of 360 Degree Brand Stewardship^{SM} quickly and eagerly, it has also been central in helping to develop the concept in the first place, and prolific in its implementation.

There would appear to be a certain logic to this fact. Asia is uniquely positioned to develop and implement the 360 Degree brand. The opportunities for broader channel development are numerous, as there is little historical baggage that ties creative ideas to just one media vehicle. But there are other, deeper reasons why Asia can lead the world in this respect.

Asia: A breeding ground for the "360 Degree Brand"

Compared to the consumer markets of North America and Europe, branding as a marketing activity, with its own service industry to support it, is a relatively new discipline in Asia. It really only started in the late 1980s and 1990s with the so-called economic miracle of the "Tiger Economies". However, Asia has more than made up for its slow start (WPP—the world's leading communications services group and Ogilvy & Mather's parent company, for example, already generates 18% of its revenue from Asia and Latin America, and predicts this will increase substantially in the next five years).

Perhaps because of its relative newness, branding in Asia represents a much more flexible and dynamic concept than in the West. Consequently, the communications agencies that have sprung up across Asia to service and develop those brands have a wonderful opportunity to develop their own ways of operating.

In the West (and indeed many agencies in Asia that adopt, rather than adapt, the traditional Western agency models), a classic ad agency is structured to produce 30-second TV commercials (TVCs) and full-page print ads. Like a factory that specializes in manufacturing just one key product, the traditional advertising agency is as bound to the TVC as a limpet is to a rock. (And the same goes for traditional direct marketing, public relations, sales promotions and other specialist single-discipline agencies.)

But it is our belief that because Asian countries tend to have a younger population and have recently begun to emerge into economic prominence, their people naturally have a more fluid and experimental approach to things (certainly, once they are set free from the stifling influence of rote learning that is characteristic of many calcified Asian education systems!).

Asian people tend overall to be highly "future-focused", exploring their options at every turn, assessing the potential of everything, always looking forward. The words "Asia" and "opportunity" are inextricably linked. By contrast, Americans tend to exist in the ever-shifting sands of the present, while Europeans are still keenly connected to their past, politically and culturally. It is noteworthy that we have found "nostalgia" to be a difficult or awkward emotion to evoke here in Asia. Sure, in Japan people hark back to the "miracle" boom years of the 1980s, but they don't want to be reminded of them. And of course, traditions still remain strong in China and other developing countries; but there is no contradiction in these countries between maintaining traditions while, at the same time, embracing enthusiastically the seismic changes that development has brought.

Fusion of influences

In addition, and partly because of the not-too-distant colonial influence in most countries, there is much fusion of influences in Asia. This fusion creates a genuine flexibility in outlook and a fluidity of thought.

Furthermore, Asians are highly adaptable, which goes some way to explaining the recurring phenomena of both "technology leapfrogging" (e.g. DVD, SMS, 3G and — in Korea — broadband penetration), and the "innovation on a theme" (which has made brands like Sony, HSBC and Samsung world-beaters).

Effectiveness of endorsement

Culturally, Asian people are also more receptive to endorsement, perhaps even more so than in other parts of the world. Asians listen, observe and — when their minds and hearts are resolved — follow. Traditional brand communications largely focus on what the brand has to say about itself. Here in Asia, however, what others say about the brand matters too. Savvy brand builders strive to understand and achieve the differential effect that endorsement can have on their success, whether that comes from a recognized expert — such as a medical professional — or from a colleague, role model or friend.

Such endorsements by default rely on non-traditional channels and "media", such as public relations, as well as trade and government relations.

Embracing 360 Degree thinking

As a result, we have found that the ability to embrace 360 Degree thinking in brand communications is indicative of Asian people's ability to perhaps embrace new ideas quicker than people in other parts of the world.

We have therefore found little difficulty in peppering this book with vivid case studies about how real brands have tackled real business problems by developing 360 Degree communications — all of which are drawn from Asian markets.

The structure of this book is straightforward. We begin by outlining why a change in how we think about brand communications is being dictated by a changing "brand environment", which makes 360 Degree thinking an imperative for anyone working in the industry today.

We then look at how this "360 Degree thinking" differs from the more classic definitions of integrated marketing, and why that fundamentally necessitates a shift in focus from "message input" (what we all used to call "the proposition" or "the button"), to orientating our thinking around a Brand Challenge. We then explore the realm of Ideas, the products of this new type of thinking.

The next four chapters then follow the logic of the development of 360 Degree brand communications. Why "Brand Loyalty" is the ultimate objective of any such communications;

why "Discovery" is a due diligence and "Insight" the vital ingredient within that; how one can create "Involvement" (which has been shown to be the only measure in Millward Brown's Link Tests that directly correlates with sales) by bringing the brand to life as an experience; and, finally, how layering and sequencing of different messages in different media at different times creates "Interplay" for a brand communications schedule, and enhances its effectiveness.

The penultimate chapter takes a look at some of the more practical aspects of 360 Degree brand building — the collaboration of different specialist disciplines, and the way in which an agency's most valuable assets — its people — need to change the way they work to deliver outstanding solutions for their clients and their brands.

Culturally unique media

The diversity of media options in Asia is truly staggering. If it moves, it's media. This is one of the more refreshing differences between this region and the West, which is often tied to a few, formulaic media such as TV, cinema, press and outdoor.

It has been fascinating to see how people across Asia have been able to apply 360 Degree branding techniques so easily. This might be due to the fact that they already live with so many media options that they have not needed to force the concept into some artificial concept of "new media".

To illustrate the breadth of media options, we have decided to highlight one unique media (note that in the language of advertising "media" denotes both singular and plural entities) from 10 countries around Asia. Each of these is briefly illustrated in a short "interlude" between each main chapter:

* Hub-caps in Singapore
* SMS texting in the Philippines
* Broadband internet in South Korea
* "i-mode" in Japan

- Wells in India
- Folk events in Sri Lanka
- Elephants in Thailand
- The Star Ferry in Hong Kong
- Puppet shows in Indonesia
- Bicycles in China

The Pacific Century

From a marketing and brand communications perspective, it is impossible to ignore the enormous creative potential the diversity of Asia provides. This region is the perfect stage on which to build great, dynamic, creative and innovative 360 Degree brands. And as we shall examine in the concluding chapter, these 360 Degree brands are set to be one of the driving forces behind what many commentators are heralding as "the Pacific Century". Those who continue to rely on one-dimensional brand communications are denying both themselves and their brands the opportunity to fulfill their true potential. As the media marketplace continues to fragment and change, such narrow-field practices are increasingly being exposed as inefficient and wasteful. Both agencies and clients alike will have to adapt if they are to survive. The times, they really are a-changing...

1

The New Brand Environment

"Come gather round people wherever you roam
and admit that the waters around you have grown
and accept it that soon you'll be drenched to the bone
if your time to you is worth savin'
then you'd better start swimming or you'll sink like a stone
for the times they are a-changing."
Bob Dylan

Once upon a time ...

It was in the 1950s and 1960s that the theory of brands and brand image evolved in the West, accompanying a period of tremendous economic growth. This was based around "the total personality of a brand, rather than any trivial product difference which decides its ultimate position in the marketplace", as David Ogilvy put it at the time.

But, it was still basically individual products or services that became brands, not corporations.

Asian corporations are typically different from Western ones in the sheer scale and diversity of their product range. Because they often grew up as trading companies and multi-purpose conglomerates, these companies have a more highly developed social role serving the community. As a result, it has historically been the companies themselves, rather than the products or services they produce, which have developed distinct personality attributes.

So much for history. Today, Western companies are busy learning corporate responsibility, while Asian companies are starting to apply many of the product and service brand-building principles learnt from the West. In many ways this convergence is a good thing, because we can now begin to move the debate on from a discussion about the differences or similarities between corporate or product brands, to *the process of branding* itself.

This is an important switch in focus, because branding is not just about packaged goods (or "fast-moving consumer goods", as they are called in some countries) — anything can be a brand these days.

What's in a name?

Let's illustrate what we mean. Of course, there are the famous packaged goods brands like Coca-Cola or Sony; but then there are also service brands such as American Express, Raffles Hotels or DHL. Then there are major entertainment brands such as Disney, or media brands such as BBC, Star TV or Nikkei. There are many people who have become brands: Michael Jordan, Ronaldo, Tiger Woods, Ichiro Suzuki have become brands through playing sport; Ralph Loren, Christian Dior, Vivienne Tam through fashion; Margaret Thatcher, Dr. Mahathir or Chairman Mao through politics; Albert Einstein and Alfred Nobel though science. Events such as the Olympics and the World Cup are brands. So are countries: we all know who makes the best wine, or the best watches or the best sushi! And so the list goes on.

The brand landscape

Not only have ideas about what constitutes a brand changed, so has the environment these brands inhabit. Brand understanding has moved on. Things have become both more complex and more sophisticated. The brand landscape has shifted dramatically.

Brand management is no longer about approving storyboards, but about managing holistic and rounded brand experiences within the public domain. To deliver a service to its clients, therefore, an agency cannot simply continue to offer partial communications solutions. Partial solutions are like an appetizer without a main course, a plate of *kai lan* without oyster sauce.

Indeed, partial solutions may do more harm than good. We ought to issue at this point a 360 Degree "Health Warning"; that brand experiences can be bad as well as good. In the past couple of years or so, Nike's reputation has been severely damaged over its employee policy in Pakistan; McDonald's was caught up in the Muslim backlash in Indonesia after September 11; and Snow Brand Foods in Japan lost all consumer trust by mislabeling ingredients. The list goes on.

360 Degree brand management requires an attention to detail, and a sure handling of all the elements that have an impact on a brand's reputation. Even the smallest considerations have a surprising impact on the overall memory bank of the consumer. Dirty counter tops, frayed carpets, poorly trained staff, the losing team you chose to sponsor, poor-quality toilet paper in the restrooms — all count for much more than the cost savings they help a brand owner to make. The point to note is that once you enter this 360 Degree brand landscape, *nothing is too large or too small* to escape being part of the "branding" process.

"Brand" is a verb, not a noun

Once this critical point is understood, the focus of the debate about what the word "brand" means also changes.

The word "brand" basically denotes a sign of ownership, and is commonly called a "trustmark". If you accept that the role of a brand is to create trust in the minds of consumers and customers, then it follows that the role of a company is "to brand" its products and services in order to make this happen.

Therefore, for those whose profession it is to build better brands, the word "brand" is better thought of as a verb rather than a noun. This is an important distinction, and one that exists right at the heart of the practice of 360 Degree marketing. For it is a complicated process "to brand" a product, a service, an event, or whatever it is you wish to brand.

At Ogilvy, we like to use the term "Brand Stewardship^SM", as it points to the need to look after the brand in all its facets: nurturing its enduring values, adapting its personality to fit with the times, re-aligning it with changing consumer habits, keeping it relevant, keeping it fresh. This, as you can imagine, is a constant challenge — especially given the paradoxical influences that constantly seek to reshape a brand's role or position.

Living with paradox

The world is full of paradoxes. Consumers want more choice and greater simplicity. They believe in brands, but are cynical about being "branded at". They are price conscious, yet gravitate towards premium brands. They respect authority figures, but reject institutionalized authority. They desire traditional family structures yet lead increasingly separate lives. They feel time-poor, but do less with the free time they have.

Similarly, there is both convergence and divergence in media. People are increasingly exposed to the same media messages and perspective on things; yet the explosion of media is leading to new and varied ways that people consume brand messages.

Just doing things better than the competition is no longer a guarantee of success. The cutting edge in markets often lies at the intersection *between* markets. Retailers are banks. Airlines are holiday companies. Car manufacturers are financiers. Sports-goods makers run theme parks. Hardware manufacturers are software consultants. This means brands have more and different competitors.

Within this world, identifying what will happen tomorrow is more important than reporting what is happening today. Brands are dynamic. They exist through the interaction of the product, the consumer and the environment. And these three dynamics are ever-changing.

Thus, the paradox for brands is that they are obliged to forge deeper and more secure relationships with their *existing* customers while simultaneously pushing out from their comfort zone to find *new* customers and *new* relationships.

A brand map

Whether brands are successful at navigating this perpetually shifting landscape is, from our experience, dependent on two things:

- how real insight into the relationship between the brand, the consumer and the environment is translated into big ideas and a meaningful brand experience
- how well they manage the relatively few loyal (what we will be calling "bonded") customers who account for the majority of profit and influence in category after category.

These are recurring themes throughout this book.

Great brands provoke their customers constantly to see the brand in a new light. They do this by identifying and owning a *big idea* that transforms the consumer landscape; by reshaping the way people see their world; by re-interpreting a product benefit; by reframing the brand ambition; or by re-igniting interest in the category.

As you go through the book, you might like to think about how the Left Bank Café brand helped reshape the way people saw their world. Or how Milo's "winning energy" and Kelvinator's "The Coolest One" campaigns re-interpreted well-understood product benefits. San Miguel Light Beer (a mere line extension) helped reframe the ambitions of the entire brand. And for examples of brands re-igniting interest in the category, look to Brand's Essence of Chicken in Asia or the "God" campaign for the churches of Singapore.

Against this backdrop, the challenge is to create brand experiences that deepen and expand the bonds between brands and their key customers and influencers.

WHAT MAKES A BRAND "BIG"?

In a recent workshop held in Kuala Lumpur with a multi-national group of senior clients from a major global brand marketing company, the team asked themselves what were the key criteria that distinguished <u>big</u> brands from ordinary ones. With the combined wisdom of some 200 years experience to draw on, it did not take too long to come up with a list of 11 major differentiators. This was the list.

A big brand:

- is "international" in scope and feel (not merely "national" or "regional")
- adds value to the experience, based on a strong product foundation
- builds from an important universal human truth (which becomes a binding agent for shared understanding of the brand)
- achieves multiple connections at various points of contact
- manages a consistent style and set of values over time and across media
- demonstrates a coherence in its marketing mix
- maintains a fresh, contemporary and recognizable look (which helps inspire a belief in the brand)
- is positive, optimistic in tone, raising the spirits of its customers
- is consistent across borders in the way it delivers the brand experience
- takes a leadership position through its actions in the marketplace, in the community and with various influential bodies
- allows people to project something of themselves onto the brand.

Remember, this was a group of experienced, hard-bitten, dyed-in-the-wool marketing men and women ... and yet, not a word about things like market share, return on investment, research & development, share of voice, distribution, leverage or price points. No, they were adamant — a <u>big</u> brand is distinguished by its ability to exert influence over the *intangible factors that underpin brand relationships*, and not by the numbers.

Establishing partnerships

360 Degree Branding® means going beyond simply "adding value" to a product proposition. It depends upon establishing a series of collaborative partnerships for the brand — with consumers, with clients, with creators of goodwill, with business partners, and with its communications agencies.

- Partnerships with consumers foster positive word of mouth.
- Partnerships with clients stimulate the necessary actions and rhetoric that support the brand within its own organization.
- Partnerships with opinion-leaders, community leaders, members of the media and other people who can create a halo of acceptance and goodwill for the brand.
- Partnerships with agencies that ensure they develop and deliver breakthrough ideas.

To achieve this, brands need thinking that goes beyond the normal agency model; and they need communications materials that go beyond conventional media boundaries.

Shaping experience — the 360 Degree mandate

360 Degree Branding® is about influencing "everything a consumer experiences". It therefore follows that agencies need to be operating in a wide and varied field of influence. In Asia, agencies can afford to be operating at nothing short of 360 Degrees.

360 Degree Branding® is more than a philosophy. It should be a way of life. In Ogilvy & Mather Asia-Pacific, we strive to:

- work in multi-discipline teams, and develop our thinking in a discipline-rich way from the start
- measure success by the integrity of our ideas, the quality of the work we produce across all points of contact, and the vitality of the brands we've helped to build

- maintain a commitment to excellence, and strive to win awards across every discipline as evidence of both our generalist outlook and our specialist expertise
- stimulate our clients to think about the forward potential of our ideas, rather than simply judge them execution by execution.

These should be, we believe, the guiding principles for anyone engaged in the pursuit of 360 Degree Branding®.

Summary

So, before we begin, let us see where we are.

We know that what it means to be a brand has changed. We know that the landscape in which brands operate has changed. And we know of the importance partnerships and experience play in developing brand relationships.

This book sets forth an altogether different understanding of brands and their communications requirements than many of the more traditional approaches. 360 Degree brand development fundamentally requires a shift in perception; it is imperative to think about a brand as a totality, and not just from one, narrow point of view — whether that is advertising or public relations, or even packaging or customer care. Only by taking a wholly inclusive point of view can truly big ideas that can deliver a genuine experience of the brand be developed and delivered to any and every point of contact.

Where to begin?

For his book *A Brand New World*, Scott Bedbury finally got to pose the big question to Starbucks' chief coffee guru Dave Olsen while out on a coffee-hunting safari in East Java: What single thing was most important to Starbucks' success? asked Bedbury, a Nike veteran who had come aboard as the roaster's chief marketing officer. Was it the coffee? The stores? The *baristas* working behind the counter?

One can imagine the faraway squint in Olsen's eye as the man Bedbury describes as "part scientist, part philosopher, part Indiana Jones" mulled the issue. Then came his answer: *"Everything matters."*

HUB-CAPS IN SINGAPORE

The free market's fast lane leaves no object unbranded. Even the humble hub-cap has become an eye-catching brand vehicle in its own right. A company in Singapore called CityDreams is busy transforming the wheels of the local taxi fleets into rolling billboards, a worldwide first when launched in January 2000.

The freewheeling hub-caps stay upright and readable at any speed, gently rocking back and forth, thanks to a specially fitted device. What once were grubby wheel caps now bear brightly painted pictures that are linked by a banner ad painted on the lower half of the cab.

This is the latest brainchild of Jayne Kwek, founder and managing director of CityDreams, the advertising arm of a Singapore taxi company called CityCab. She also came up with the innovative idea of using taxi-roof ads and wholly painted taxi ads. Kwek argues that this "total vehicle advertising solution" is both good business and good fashion. The hub-caps, she says, "dress up the taxis like buttons on a suit". Cab drivers are in favor of this new medium too — they say it makes their cabs look smarter, and they say people on the sidewalks just can't take their eyes off them.

Many Singapore taxis now have hub-cap media messages

2

The 360 Degree Imperative

"Twenty-first century marketing will mean bringing a brand to life for <u>all</u> its constituencies, using all possible contact points, and not simply relying on old formulas."
Sir Martin Sorrell, Chairman, WPP

Practising what you preach

360 Degree brand communications is the only logical response to the changing brandscape in Asia. It is not a new idea. Nor is it exclusively the preserve of one or two agencies. Every day, we read about big ad agencies "tearing down the walls between disciplines", championing the brand through multiple media channels. And, in addition to the term "360 Degree brand communications", we hear of "total branding", "communications optimization" and "media wholism".

As we know, however, it is much easier to talk about such things in presentations and meetings than it is to turn it into a cohesive, *functioning* reality. To create a truly 360 Degree business, an agency will need to utterly transform itself — physically and philosophically.

Branding past and future

Most will be familiar with the history of "branding". From the earliest days of putting the name of a wholesaler on sacks of tea or the "brand" of the farmer on herds of cattle, brand communications was about finding media opportunities to advertise the reputation of a manufacturer, owner or distributor. From about 1900 onwards, following the industrial revolution, the golden age of the research & development-driven "product breakthrough" emerged, cleaning whites whiter, ridding people of indigestion, or supplying fortifying breakfast cereals. After the Second World War, manufacturers began a more systematic process of understanding consumer wants (not just needs), and so began a creative revolution that set out to excite and entice people to buy things which were not strictly commodities.

In the second half of the 20th century, numerous voices rose up and began challenging brands, their claims and their corporate behavior. In the immortal words of John Finley Dunne, a new tribe of journalists strove to "comfort the afflicted and afflict the comfortable". Beyond the influence of reporters, unions pressed for workers' rights and activists advocated such causes as health and the environment. Consumers listened. Companies heard. Brand owners began to think about actions and policies consistent with the promises they sought to deliver. Not surprisingly, it was during these decades that public relations grew into a multi-billion-dollar, global industry.

And now the Internet revolution has begun to change the way we brand things in the new millennium. Satisfying consumer wants is no longer a simple process. The complicated world we live in means that we in the branding business are increasingly being forced to invent new ways of thinking about brands, and even new business models, just to survive.

New business model

The implications for a corporate strategy are clear:
  i)   a glorious past does not guarantee a golden future
  ii) how a company behaves says more about it than what it says

iii) companies with a varied portfolio of offerings increase their "future options" to take advantage of ongoing changes in the marketplace.

One way of looking at a model of business evolution is to map the various product or service options according to how difficult it is/was to introduce the new service on one axis, against the amount of leverage it will provide in adding value to clients on the other.

Figure 2.1 shows some of the initiatives that Ogilvy & Mather Asia-Pacific has taken in this regard in the past five years.

Figure 2.1: Evolution at Ogilvy Asia-Pacific

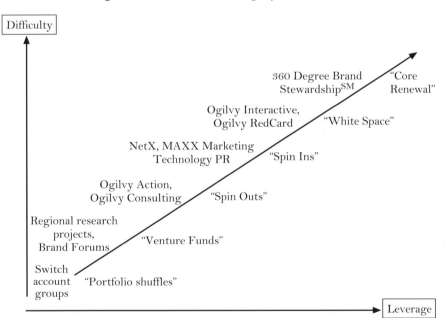

Note: the "Difficulty vs Leverage" concept and the six categories of new business model are taken from Gary Hamel and the lectures accompanying his book *Leading the Revolution.*

Reasons to believe

Clearly, introducing a 360 Degree business model is never going to be easy. But we also know how important it is to do so; we have already seen how brands and media have changed irrevocably. And we have seen why the appearance of 360 Degree brand-building agencies is therefore the natural and logical conclusion of this changed environment. So while it may be a difficult transition to make, it is also a necessary one.

There are other reasons too. Many traditional agency groups consist of a collection of "sister agencies", each offering a different service. Each operates in what amounts to splendid isolation, barely speaking to one another, let alone collaborating. The danger of *not* having a cohesive 360 Degree brand positioning is that a marketing services group becomes a series of mere implementation agencies, each being pushed further and further downstream.

Upstream, we see the management consultants turning their steely gaze on brands and marketing. "Marketing is too important to be left to brand managers," reads one Bain report. While this may be an exaggeration of a particular point of view, the fact is that few traditional disciplines in the brand communications industry have a handle in the boardroom. Public Relations and brand-identity companies do to an extent. This tends to arise in relation to M&A activity (mergers and acquisitions), crisis management, internal communications, CEO media training, public affairs and corporate identity, all of which affect trust in businesses and their brands.

In order to secure this kind of access across a broader range of offerings, there is clearly a need to convince clients that agencies are once again pushing the boundaries, and really are at the cutting edge of their field — and, more importantly, that they are capable of taking a broader business-oriented perspective. Here in the Asia-Pacific region, we have found that the Ogilvy & Mather 360 Degree Brand Stewardship^{SM} philosophy has been instrumental in re-opening access to senior clients and re-engaging with them as business partners.

360 Degree vision

A truly 360 Degree agency has a number of "needs": to cross borders — real and imagined; to challenge our industry's comfort zones; to deliver solutions that reach not only into consumers' lives, but back into the factories themselves; and to be building brand equity into every facet of a client's organization that affects the end-customer's impression of its brand.

To achieve this, we need deeper insight; broader ideas; better execution; greater influence and endorsement; employees that <u>live</u> the brand; more-involving delivery; and tougher evaluation.

Only in this way, we believe, will we build brands that can reach their full potential.

To achieve all this, we always try to remember the following:

- that we are in the knowledge business; and that we must therefore own and disseminate better and more insightful knowledge
- that we are in the ideas business; and that we therefore need to deliver better, bigger and more sophisticated ideas
- that we are in the brand business; and that to stay in this business, we will need more influence on the total brand, which will mean more influence on all the myriad things that shape it.

What is 360 Degree brand communication?

It is something very simple. It is an approach to marketing that sees no limits on the number of contact points possible with a target consumer — media will be found, and activities created, to maximize involvement with the brand, whenever and wherever they are needed most. In other words, it starts with the problem, and then tailors the solution to solve it.

If this sounds obvious, think about how conventional agencies approach things. From their point of view, *the solutions are pre-fixed*. Not only that, those solutions are limited by the number of media they are able or prepared to deal in. A client's problem can then only be addressed via those conventional channels. The problem, effectively, comes second to the solution: media selections are already predetermined before the business problems are addressed. As the saying goes: "To a man with a hammer, every problem looks like a nail."

This is the antithesis of 360 Degree communications development. To reiterate: a 360 Degree communications approach *starts* with the problem — or the Brand Challenge — and then finds the media and messages that best answer that problem. It may be that the answers aren't "advertising" at all — but staff training, or public relations, or better distribution networks. This is what makes a 360 Degree approach to brands and business so refreshing.

Decisively different

Perhaps the difference between a 360 Degree approach and a conventional approach can be summed up like this: conventional agencies exist whereas a 360 Degree brand communications agency exists *to deliver solutions to all sorts of surprising problems in all sorts of surprising ways*.

As dictated by its simple logic of "brand problem first, communications solution second", 360 Degree brand communication has to place the identification of that problem, and the ideas to solve it, ahead of media selection. It is therefore, by default, media-neutral — a rare thing even today.

Questions and answers

What do you want to achieve with your brand communications? What precisely is the problem you are trying to address? What part of your brand equity is causing the block? What are the long-term ambitions for the brand? Who and *where* are your target customers?

It is hard to see how any discussion of media selection can possibly take place without having first addressed all of these types of strategic issues and without having thoroughly immersed the brand team in the lives and habits of the target consumer.

The tools of the trade

In order to harness each discipline's expertise and channel it, there are a number of tools we use at Ogilvy & Mather Asia-Pacific to create alignment of understanding within the team. They act as a shared platform for the team, a kind of operating system, from which each discipline's specific programs can be launched.

- Brand Scan: an assessment of all the strengths and weaknesses the brand has, arranged on six equities. This effectively produces a "health check" on the brand: where do its biggest opportunities and problems lie?
- Brand Audit: an exhaustive effort to set down, in black and white, the intangible cluster of feelings, impressions, connections, opinions, flashes of memory, hopes and satisfactions, criticisms and disappointments which blend together to form the customer's perception of the brand.
- BrandPrint: a succinct set of words that reflect the unique relationship the brand has with its customers (often accompanied, but never supplanted, by visuals, sounds or other sensory stimulus to evoke this "sense" of the brand).
- Points of Contact: a process of immersion to assess all the encounters the customer has with the brand, and identify the ideal time, place, behavior and attitude of mind to involve the brand in the life of the customer.

This is just one agency's toolkit. Each may have its own. But essentially the underlying requirement is four-fold: to interrogate, to understand, to define, and to disseminate.

First step: Interrogate the context

To understand the opportunities, we must first identify the problems, by conducting a "health check" on the brand. We assess all the strengths and weaknesses (but particularly the weaknesses) that a brand faces against each of six equities to identify the biggest issues facing the brand as it seeks to win in the marketplace.

- How well is the product performance supporting the brand?
- How strong and engaging is the brand's image?
- How strong is the brand's customer franchise?
- How well is the brand leveraged in the trade environment?
- Does the brand present a clear, consistent and differentiating presence?
- To what extent is the brand endorsed internally, and by influencers and the communities in which it lives?

Second step: Unearth the relationship

If our aim is to define, distill and express the unique relationship between the brand and its customers, we first have to unearth a true understanding of the emotional elements that make up that relationship. This is not easy to achieve, when brands are built on layers of different benefits:

- tangible product features, such as its price, style, size
- rational benefits, such as being thirst-quenching, energy-boosting, or providing speed of service, and so on
- emotional benefits, such as making you feel more excited, stylish or indulged
- psychological benefits, such as making you feel more secure, intelligent or self-assured.

And behind all these are the personal memories or associations a consumer has of a brand. Or, to put it another way, the personal memories or associations the brand has *created* in the hearts and minds of consumers.

American Express is not just a piece of plastic. Year after year in focus groups, it is amazing how vocal people are willing to be when talking about their American Express card. They remember the first day they got their card. They talk evocatively about how it made them feel like they had "arrived"; that they were part of an exclusive group; and that in some very important, personal way, it represented a reward for their struggle on the road to success in their lives.

How do users really *feel* about your brand? This is not a straightforward exercise. You can't get this kind of intangible insight from the usual quantitative research. Nor can you just bluntly ask a consumer how she feels about her ice cream or computer, or what is her relationship with toilet paper or detergent. We are not looking for superficial platitudes or preferences. So, instead, we use a wide variety of interactive interviewing techniques designed to unearth the hidden, emotional truth of the brand, to gain true insight into the brand–consumer relationship. We ask questions like: "How does the brand make you feel about yourself? What sensory images trigger the brand? What memories or emotions does the brand evoke?"

Third step: Define the brand's DNA

From this host of contextual and qualitative evaluation, we cull the insight needed to create what we call the BrandPrint. This is a succinct set of words that reflect the brand in its totality, the way it represents itself in the world. This is its absolute, unique core — its best and purest qualities, its DNA.

This helps us unleash the power of the brand. Once the core of the brand can be articulated, we can then liberate it through *all* forms of communication — not just advertising. Every form of communication (which occurs each time the brand comes into contact with its consumer) must be true to the BrandPrint. From front desk to brochure, from product placement to PR, every point of contact must reflect that brand's DNA.

Some examples: the Ogilvy BrandPrint for American Express is:

"American Express is not for everyone. It is for those who think bigger thoughts, do bigger things and paint bigger pictures."

For *The Economist* it is articulated thus:

"*The Economist* is red and prestigious — it commands respect wherever it is aired.

Intelligent, influential and insightful, with no room for mediocrity, *The Economist* attracts those who hold similar qualities dear."

Fourth step: Taking the brand into the world

In order to harness each discipline's expertise and channel it, we need to have a very precise point of focus that all branches of communications can work to: the key *Brand Challenge*. This represents the single, most fundamental issue all communications activities must address. The Challenge gives direction to all brand communications, and is the spark for developing a *Brand Idea*.

Of course, for multi-layered, multi-channel, cross-discipline communications to work in a cohesive manner, there needs to be a single, big brand idea; an idea that can be brought to life in different media, in different ways, for different stakeholders. But note: an idea is not simply a logo. A brand idea is bigger, more complex, more varied, and more *interesting* than a simple graphic device. Nike is a lot more than just a swoosh!

Summary

This chapter has sought to show how and why 360 Degree brand thinking will become an imperative for all agencies in the future. And as part of that rationale, we have shown how such thinking fundamentally differs from a conventional (old-fashioned) approach to brand communications. And finally, we have outlined the basic shape that 360 Degree brand development takes within one particular agency.

360 Degree brand thinking clearly offers marketers a better and a more effective means for building equity and driving sales. But don't just take our word for it! Here are the words of Shelly Lazarus, Chairman Ogilvy & Mather Worldwide, from a recent speech given to some of America's most senior CEOs and corporate chairmen.

SHELLY LAZARUS ON 360 DEGREE BRAND STEWARDSHIP[SM]

"Given the turmoil and tumult of the marketplace in recent years, brand marketers face some unique challenges. We have had waves of globalization, the tech run-up, media exploding, converging and then diverging. Then we had the dot-com boom (which I have heard referred to as 'hype and hope on steroids'), and then a spectacular and unforgiving bust. And now we are left with the gloomy shadows of recession.

Out of chaos has come great opportunity to build brands far more deeply, more effectively. The great debate about the value of brands is over. Finished. Everybody wants a strong brand and everybody knows that a strong brand is what it takes to succeed — to be profitable, to build market share and secure customer loyalty, to face down rivals, to move into new markets and across borders, and to remain relevant to the ever-fickle consumer. Building a brand is not just a 'nice thing to do'. It's not just what some of those 'consumer' companies do. It's no longer 'fluffy'. It's smart. And it's essential. Bottom line, in today's world, you have to have a strong brand to succeed.

But to build a strong brand, you must also have a keen sense of 'branding'. The brand is really only what is created in the hearts and minds of consumers. What is important to recognize is that this relationship is neither simple, nor simply created. This relationship is built on all the experiences your consumers have of the brand, all the information and knowledge, all the contacts with the brand, direct and inadvertent, that add up over time.

To quote Jeremy Bullmore, a brilliant marketing thinker, 'Consumers build brands like birds build nests, from scraps and straws they chance upon.'

The more we focus on the importance of the brand, the more we become acutely aware of the overwhelming need for the 360 Degree Brand Experience. Scraps and straws add up to the most valuable asset a company has.

Therein lies our opportunity — our ability to capitalize on a myriad of contacts that build the relationship. We just have to want to. We have to have the will and the imagination to move beyond the way we've always done it, and to try ways that have never been tried."

(Extract from a speech by Shelly Lazarus, Chairman of Ogilvy & Mather Worldwide)

SMS Texting In The Philippines

If you are still in need of further evidence that technology can change the world, consider what happened in the Philippines in January 2001. Thousands of Filipinos, unhappy with their corrupt government, took to the streets to demonstrate against President Joseph Estrada, ultimately forcing him to resign. And it was SMS text messages, sent from one mobile phone to another, or from one handset to many others, that played the key role in stimulating and organizing the protest. It began with political jokes spreading like wildfire, jokes that undermined Estrada's credibility; it ended with SMS messages that rallied and mobilized huge numbers of people out onto the street, messages that spread the word on where demonstrations were being held. Texting has changed the way we live, love, and topple governments.

The Philippines ranks around 40th in GDP per capita. But it ranks number 1 — way ahead of most developed nations — in one element of advanced wireless communications: SMS text messaging. Traditionally a follower in technology rather than a leader, the Philippines is actually the SMS capital of the world, a veritable texting phenomenon. Despite the fact that mobile-phone penetration is nowhere near that of the developed nations in Western Europe and North America, the Philippines single-handedly generates more text messages than all of Europe combined. With over 150 million messages transmitted each day, the Philippines is turning out to be one of the most networked countries in the world.

Initially, messaging services were free. Now, given the explosion in usage, network operators have had to introduce a token text message charge to encourage "responsible text messaging". This has done little to dampen the enthusiasm for mobile messaging — there are almost twice as many cell phones as landline telephones.

Of course, the low cost of SMS communication is part of the attraction. But there is also a deeper cultural reason that explains why text messaging is so big in the Philippines. Extended families are ubiquitous, and they include not just grandparents, but aunts, uncles and cousins. Filipinos even count third cousins as close family. Extended families represent an important support system, and society puts a high premium on social relations. When the atomizing tendencies of urbanization threaten these previously tight-knit community and kinship ties, SMS keeps families, neighbors, and friends connected.

SMS has become an effective media channel. Although it is a simple, low-tech feature of a phone, SMS has been used by Filipino operators to offer nearly as wide a range of services as Japanese operators currently offer with 2.5G. Services include daily news and soap-opera updates, games, lotteries, m-commerce applications (purchasing from vending machines), and limited mobile banking. The most popular application is a monthly quiz/lottery in which subscribers are sent three trivia questions daily, each via a separate SMS. Filipino operators now get 27% of their revenue from data applications.

3

Integration Redefined

"Symphonic composition is simply the mastery of multi-channel competency."
Jeff Blake, symphony conductor

In the mid 1990s, "Integration" was the catchword on the lips of agencies, clients, and marketing consultants the world over. But now it has become a pejorative term. We are not sure why or how, but it has. Perhaps it was the difficulties of combining the different cultures of different brand communications disciplines in those days. Or perhaps it comes from a resurgence of "advertising arrogance". Or perhaps it is a word that has simply gone out of fashion. Whatever it is, and whatever has caused it, "integration" is certainly out of favor.

Most likely, it is the pervasive and narrow implementation of so-called integrated campaigns that has counted so heavily against it. The approach so often taken to demonstrate "integration" has, quite rightly, been seen as flawed, and thus the entire concept has been tainted.

But this is wrong. As any marketer will tell you, getting the different media to work to an integrated brand-activity plan is absolutely crucial to the success of any brand. But it requires a new body of thinking to demonstrate how this can be a powerful and creative exercise, rather than the "painting by numbers" with which the word "integration" has become associated.

Integration redefined

360 Degree brand communications is a new form of integration. It brings different disciplines into play, to work together to enhance both efficiency and effectiveness. For the purposes of this chapter, we shall be exploring the differences between what we call "old-style integration" and new-style 360 Degree communications. And if we can rescue the word "integration" from its negative associations along the way, so much the better.

The old mantra

The old mantra was "consistency" — consistency of message, of target and, more often than not, of medium. How this manifested itself was through a rather predictable and insistent emphasis on "creative consistency", whereby key images (usually taken from the TV commercial) were replicated throughout other media channels and marketing collateral. This practice of "replication" was passed off as "integration" for quite some time. But it is a model that cannot work in the current, media-rich, channel-fragmented world that brands now compete in.

Brand consistency

While some sense of creative or thematic consistency is obviously important, this narrow view of "integration"' (based on "creative consistency") is an insufficient response to the complexity of brand–consumer interaction in today's world. The bigger concept driving successful 360 Degree brand communications programs today is "brand consistency".

Breadth of activity is vital to building brands and businesses today. And only brand consistency can provide a sufficiently firm foundation from which multiple and diverse brand communications activities can take flight.

This has several implications: firstly, there is no reason why different messages might not be used to target different audiences via different media, so long as those communications are aligned to meeting a common brand goal, and are in tune with brand values and personality.

Secondly, this also means that any medium can be an appropriate brand communications vehicle. Previous attempts at integration relied on visual or aural consistency, which simply limited a brand to visual or aural channels. Brand experiences can and do live beyond these channels.

Thirdly, it takes away the need to build a communications program around a single medium (such as TV); which is just as well, as the fragmentation of media channels means that mass communication can no longer be taken for granted. Each medium can now be looked at both independently (how effectively it is working) and as part of the whole (how it is contributing to campaign resonance).

And finally, it allows for the triumph of the "idea" over the "image". Big brand *ideas*, and not just pleasant art direction, are the drivers of brand consistency. Ideas create and sustain brands, and 360 Degree communications is in the business of producing them.

Flexibility and resonance

With multiple activities, control is enhanced. Imagine a graphic equalizer on your media programming — the ability to turn up or turn down various elements, depending on the current situation. Such an option was impossible under old-style, linear integration.

Multiple ideas and activities across disciplines combine in ways that bring resonance and, therefore, greater impact to brand communications. Resonance is far more powerful than repetition for creating consumer involvement. Brand consistency allows for a level of interplay between communications activities that "old-style integration" (based, as it was, on repetition) could not.

Compare and contrast

Perhaps the best way to illustrate the differences between the two approaches is to look at the language of integration as opposed to the language of 360 Degree communications. By exploring the nuances and connotations of the terminology, it is possible to tease out the characteristics of each.

What we can see from this comparison of vocabulary is that the language of integration is all about *cyclical repetition*. The

Figure 3.1   The old mantra vs the new

The Language of Integration	The Language of 360 Degree
1. **Consistent**: compatible; in harmony; constant	1. **Flexible**: pliable; adaptable; versatile
2. **Single-minded**: with one aim or purpose; a narrow concentration	2. **Contextual**: where the environment of a message helps determine its exact meaning; when a message is beneficially influenced by the situation in which it is found
3. **Distinct**: separate; disconnected; set apart	3. **Fusion**: a fusing or melding together; a blending; a bringing together
4. **Hierarchy**: (from the Greek *heiros* (sacred) + *archos* (ruler)): organized and arranged in order of traditional rank, grade and authority	4. **Matrix** (from Latin *mater* (mother)): that from within which something originates, takes form — thus to create; to invent; to begin
5. **Replication**: an exact copy of something that's gone before; a close copy of an original	5. **Resonance**: the effect produced when the natural vibration frequency of a body is amplified by vibrations from another body
6. **Impact**: (verb) to force tightly together; a striking together; the force of a collision; a shock	6. **Involvement** (from Latin *volvere* (to roll)): being entangled and ensnared; being included; active participation
7. **Repetition**: a copy; (to repeat) to say again; to recite; to re-broadcast over and over	7. **Interplay**: the enhanced effect created when one thing interacts, or comes into contact, with another

language of 360 Degree communications highlighted in Figure 3.1, however, is more about *diversity and fertility*.

With cyclical repetition, once an "idea" has been decided upon, process and logistics become the dominant activity. Idea-generation sessions are few and far between. If ideas are the life-blood of brands, then this system would bleed a brand dry.

On the other hand, the "diversity and fertility" of 360 Degree brand communications encourages a perpetually creative culture. Media opportunities are open-ended. Idea-generation is ongoing. Everyone is empowered to think "ideas, ideas, ideas".

A firm foundation

This "new-style integration" will only work if it is based on a clear and shared understanding of what the brand (and its communications) needs to stand for; and a common objective (or Challenge) from which to derive ideas for communications activities.

- **Brand DNA**
  It is critical to establish and identify some expression of brand DNA (what, within a brand, is immutable, cannot be transgressed, and which signals this brand — and this brand only — within its competitive set). Without an expression of such core identification factors, ideas cannot be rooted in brand values. Brand consistency would be impossible.

- **A central Brand Challenge**
  Similarly, there needs to be one single organizing function which galvanizes and controls the output of brand activity, which can serve not only as a brief, but also as a criterion against which to judge the validity of communications programs.

  The Brand Challenge becomes the single most important feature of 360 Degree communications. A weak Challenge will lead to a weak implementation program. A well-defined

Challenge will produce an enhanced set of brand activities. The tighter the Challenge, the easier it is to produce focused and effective communications activities.

Some concluding implications

The 360 Degree approach begins and ends with the *points of contact* that a customer has with the brand. It doesn't begin or end with all the specialist *disciplines* that work on the brand. The customer does not distinguish between disciplines — in fact, most will lump all commercially inspired messages together as "advertising".

It is important to note that 360 Degree Branding® is not about amassing all the forces in one great big World-War-One-style push. Not *every* campaign requires *every* discipline's contribution at *every* stage of the campaign. Indeed, there are plenty of examples throughout this book where 360 Degree campaigns only use two or three disciplines in the entirety of a campaign. The point is not to use all the disciplines, but to think through *which* of all the available disciplines will make the biggest contribution, in tandem with others, to the benefit of the overall brand Idea.

Saying that, there are some practical lessons we have learnt over the past few years in facilitating the learning and cooperation process:

- Different specialist disciplines need to come together and coexist under one roof. The more isolated the different functions are, the less likely they are to function well together. Idea-generation will suffer. Opportunities for idea-fusion, resonance and cross-fertilization will be missed.
- The model of "top down" creativity from the Advertising Department needs to be re-thought, as does the supremacy of advertising-only creative awards systems. Some of the most creative implementation programs in the world are being

produced in non-traditional formats, yet go undetected by the conventional, TV, and print-dominated awards systems.

- Agencies need to restructure internally to create a forum of ideas that encourages a real meritocracy, where ideas are valued from every quarter. Brands know no limits to the multiplicity of their interactions with consumers. Similarly, agencies need to encourage the unrestricted free-flow of ideas.
- Cross-disciplinary talent must be fostered. Any brand needs a champion that can work comfortably in any medium and any discipline, that can assess and arbitrate ideas and messages so as to protect the brand from miscommunication and off-strategy ideas.

An excellent example of the power of true 360 Degree brand thinking and delivery is the following case study from Singapore.

CASE STUDY 1

Making the Omniscient omnipresent — the "God" campaign from Singapore

Background

Singapore is a truly multicultural society, where Hindu, Buddhist, Muslim, Taoist, and Christian communities all happily coexist. But it is also a city well-known for its secular priorities — they say that Singapore's national sport is shopping.

The "Love Singapore Movement" — a group of 150 Christian churches — wanted to increase the awareness of God and, uniquely, they were prepared to use and pay for mass media to do so.

The Objective

They wanted to create "God consciousness"; that is, to raise the top-of-mind awareness of God amongst Singaporeans as they went about their lives.

31

But there were two important caveats — to avoid creating a campaign that could be seen as evangelical, as a recruitment drive; and to approach the campaign in a manner that made Christianity seem fresh, relevant, and contemporary.

The Block

The Christian God has an image problem.

He has an antiquated brand image — old fashioned, out of touch, a piece of ancient history. He is felt to be overbearing and authoritarian — a dictatorial rule-maker who is swift to punish. Worse still, He is seen as distant and unapproachable, difficult to talk to and unwilling to listen.

The Brand Challenge

The Challenge was to perform an "image-job" on God, to transform Him from "killjoy schoolmaster" to someone you would want to invite out with your friends.

The Insight

God is Everywhere. So are the media opportunities.

If we could create a campaign that used unusual and surprising 360 Degree media, God's voice could call out to people in unusual and startlingly refreshing ways. Not only would this bring God into focus at exactly the most appropriate times and places, it would automatically position God as a contemporary, up-to-date, forward-thinking "early adopter" who embraced new media.

The Brand Idea

Give God a personality. God speaks in His own voice, directly to you. This is not the God you imagined. He is irreverent and witty. He is someone you enjoy having around. He is attractive. God has a sense of humor; He loves life. God is the sort of person you'd like to get to know more about.

The Work — How God spoke ...

"His voice calls out to me in so many ways ..."

"God is Everywhere and in Everything" … ambient media

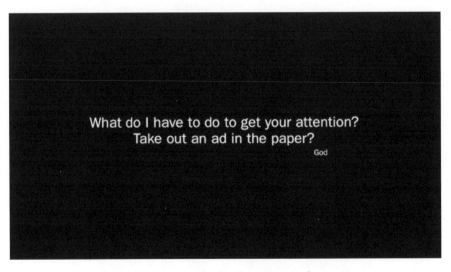

"He is in my head…" … print media

"And in my heart..." ... online media

"And in my hand..." ... SMS cellphone media

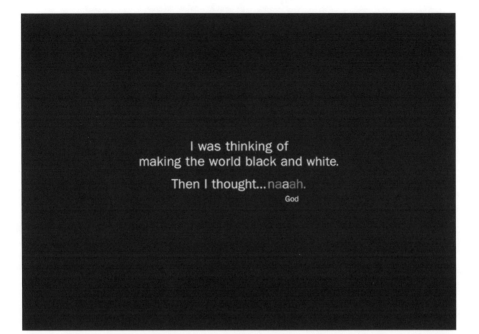

"He appeareth before mine eyes…" … TV media

"And is there where I least expect…" … Web banners

"I am surrounded by His Name..." ... outdoor and bus-side media
(Reproduced with kind permission of the "Love Singapore Movement")

Results

God (and His campaign) is talked about on the street, over the airwaves, and over the dinner table. God is back on the agenda. The public was given the opportunity to receive SMS messages from God. Some 11,600 people registered for the service. Some 1.2 million free postcards were taken away. The campaign has won seven Gold Lions at Cannes (so far...).

BROADBAND INTERNET IN SOUTH KOREA

There are not many countries in the world where "ADSL" is a household term. Yet it is in South Korea, which has the highest broadband penetration rate in the world.

ADSL stands for Asymmetrical Digital Subscriber Line, a technology that exploits unused frequencies on copper telephone lines to transmit traffic, typically at multi-megabit speeds. ADSL can allow voice and high-speed data to be sent simultaneously over the same line. Because the service is "always available", end-users don't need to dial-in or wait for call set-up. It can deliver up to six megabits of data per second, which is up to 120-times faster than dial-up service and 100-times faster than ISDN.

Broadband is important technology, because it allows new applications such as online transactions, voice/music/video streaming, interactive online gaming, TV telephone, remote office, and e-learning. Many as-yet unknown applications are currently in development.

South Korea leads the world in both the usage and development of broadband infrastructure. By the end of 2001, 13.9% of its population were hooked up to ADSL broadband. This is a remarkable figure, especially when compared to equivalent penetrations around the world — 3.2% in the U.S. (the country that gave birth to the Internet), 0.9% in Japan and 0.8% in the entire European Union.

By March 2002, the total number of South Korean broadband Internet subscribers was over 8.3 million, and is expected to exceed 10 million by the end of the year. Forty per cent of all households have a broadband Internet connection.

Why is all this talk of speed important to brand marketers? Simply because broadband Internet users go online more often and for longer than their dial-up counterparts: in fact, they go online three-times as often, and spend four-times as long online, accessing over twice as many pages (source: Nielsen/NetRatings). The average South Korean spends 16 hours a month on the Internet and runs through 96 pages in a session that averages 45 minutes. By comparison, the average American is online for 10 hours per month, going through just 37 pages in a typical 32-minute session. *South Koreans are surfing at twice the speed of their American counterparts*, and because their Internet experience is so enhanced by being so fast, they are surfing wider and for longer.

Broadband, which has been deemed the true "eight-lane superhighway of information", provides a backbone infrastructure for all industries; it is an infrastructure that supplies information and knowledge and, more importantly, it creates value. Consequently, while the rest of the world flounders in the after-effects of a "dot-bomb", South Korea is enjoying a flourishing Internet-based economy. Businesses such as online games, animation and online trading services have blossomed. And with their broadband Internet service management know-how and experience, major Korean IT corporations and related businesses such as communications equipment manufacturers, and content and solution providers continue to expand into overseas markets. As a result, the proportion of the IT industry against the GDP rose from 8.6% in 1997 to 12.9% in 2001. The South Korean IT industry has become a major engine which fuels the national economy.

Just how has South Korea managed to become the strongest broadband Internet nation on earth in such a short period of time? The answer lies with a far-sighted government IT policy, a competitive telecommunications environment and low telecom tariffs. One key influence was the fact that over 90% of all households were located within a four-kilometer radius of the local telephone offices. This meant an easy transition to ADSL provision.

Furthermore, cultural factors played a critical role. The Korean population is young, averaging in the early 30s. They are well educated and literate, and technology had already been integrated into their culture in many different ways. Already proficient in text messaging by cell phone, and having mastered various other technologies for keeping in touch, participating actively in online communities was second nature. Broadband's ability to readily add music, photos and home movies into the mix has become a Korean "killer app" — broadband makes the virtual experience so much more vivid.

For brand marketers in Korea, it means that the Internet channel has always been seen as a viable medium from day one, unlike in other markets where slow speeds on the "World Wide Wait" have limited opportunities for brand communications. According to the *Wall Street Journal*, South Korea is using the Internet "more effectively and efficiently than any other market in the world". Furthermore, it is able to reach a broad spectrum of user-groups, not just the youth segment; research shows that the number of broadband users in their 30s and 40s is growing rapidly, and will soon surpass the youth segment.

Of course, in Korea (like elsewhere) online games are very popular among young people. But broadband *as a medium* is having a much wider effect on consumers' lives: it is widely used in education, from elementary school up to university level. And it is being increasingly used in the fields of media and personal transaction; there are already 750 Internet broadcasting stations in Korea, and cyber stock-trading accounts for an incredible 71% of total monthly trading volumes. Furthermore, the variety of content that users can now enjoy is vast and sophisticated — the days of simple search-engine utilization are long gone. Korean broadband has ushered in a new standard for self-servicing interactivity that includes e-commerce, gaming, banking, financing, and news.

So, where next for the most advanced Internet nation on earth? The answer is, wireless broadband, where vast and fast content can be downloaded without even having to hook up any connecting wires. The South Korean government is expanding the penetration of the 3G (third generation) wireless Internet network to 90% of the population. This will enable the workforce to handle large volumes of data or multi-media content while on the move. This will include capacity for data communication at low prices in public places, such as subway stations and airports, a development that will keep South Korea ahead of the rest of the world for some time to come.

4

Orientating Around a Brand Challenge

"A compass is useless without a course to steer by."
Joshua Slocum, *Sailing Alone Around the World*

It is not without good reason that Sun Tzu's *The Art of War* is one of the best-selling business strategy books of all time. The competitive nature of business makes it ripe for analogy with the ultimate competitive scenario — military combat. Tactics, strategy, positioning, planning, intelligence, gains and losses — all form part of the daily dialogue of business, and, particularly in Marketing, where brand warfare is the name of the game.

For the purposes of understanding a fully 360 Degree approach to brand marketing, a military analogy is very useful (perhaps it is no coincidence that one major agency network refers to it as "Total Branding", echoing the German term for Total War — *blitzkrieg*).

One aspect of battle strategy is particularly pertinent to our discussion here; namely, the vision to use the vast resources and firepower that are available, efficiently and effectively. For the D-Day landings in Normandy in the Second World War, the Allied Commanders had 42 different specialist divisions to coordinate. At Ogilvy & Mather Asia-Pacific, there are 18 different communications disciplines to work with.

How, then, to best coordinate them? By what organizing principle can we harness their expertise to make sure each division is delivering materials and programs that work for the greater benefit of the brand? There has to be some common goal that can bring the different efforts together.

Setting objectives

In every brand manager's marketing plans there are a series of business objectives that he or she is required to deliver against: achieve 15% sales growth, gain 3% market share by end of Year One, drive levels of brand awareness to 95%, deliver 50% penetration amongst all 16–25-year-olds.

The objective is the end destination. It provides a clear vision of where the business and the brand need to be. It provides a benchmark for evaluating performance over time. It provides management and shareholders with a clear sense of financial direction and strategy.

Delivering the strategy

Being able to deliver what we preach is what makes us accountable. It doesn't matter whether single, dual or multiple disciplines are used. But, putting a strategy together into a coherent and consistent communications program requires some discipline.

Before we start, we need to make sure we don't waste time chasing down impossible opportunities. It is vital to understand the basic principles of strategy.

There are only four core strategies, as several celebrated business school writers have demonstrated: defend, attack, outflank, employ guerilla tactics. But, all are not options in all cases. Each one is right for a particular type of brand, and the wrong strategy for other types of brands. Here is a simple checklist of when each may be put to good use.

DEFENSE	ATTACK
Dominant brand leader	*Strong # 2 or 3 brand*
Consolidate market	Grow brand share
Attack your own weaknesses	Attack the weakest point of the leader's strength (rather than the leader's "weakness" — this will not be important territory)
Block every strong move	
Monitor every move	
Strike back with counter-measures	
Keep something in reserve	Keep the front narrow
Smooth things over to keep the market stable	Don't rely on one point of attack forever

OUTFLANK	GUERILLA TACTICS
Weak mainstream brand	*Niche brand*
Grow share in one sector	Find a gap in the market
Move into an uncontested area	Identify a territory small enough to defend
Follow through — the pursuit is as important as the initial maneuver	Never act like a leader, or fight a lost cause
Keep forces concentrated	Be narrow and deep in focus
	Develop alliances

Objective vs Challenge

However, setting the objective does nothing to help us gather together different disciplines in a way that allows them to work in a cohesive fashion. An objective ignores the concept of brand. It ignores the role of the consumer and takes no account of how this objective can be achieved.

There are a million ways of achieving an objective. But there is only one way to harness different brand specialists to work together to achieve a common goal. We call this the Brand Challenge.

By placing an objective in front of a specialist, the solution is always predictable; it will come from that specialist's area of expertise. However, we find that by defining a Brand Challenge, the solution-finding becomes naturally *media neutral* and *media rich*. Specialists begin to work together in a cohesive way.

The difference between an objective and a Challenge is simple:

> *In order to achieve "this" (objective), we have to do "that" (challenge).*

An objective defines a destination. The Challenge describes the essential barrier a team needs to overcome to get there.

Thus a Challenge is highly focused, action-specific, and something that helps you achieve your objective. It helps us redefine the way people experience a brand.

Some examples

- **Milo (Thailand)**

    Objective: To become the #1 tonic drink by becoming more relevant to the lives of Thai kids, particularly in rural areas.

    Challenge: Make kids feel that Milo can help them fulfill their sporting dreams.

- **Left Bank Café (Taiwan)**

    Objective: To create a new ready-to-drink coffee brand targeted at young women which sells at a large price premium.

    Challenge: Make the experience of the brand as sophisticated and artistic in real life as it is in the dreams of its customers.

- **Sampoerna A Mild (Indonesia)**

    Objective: To revive the brand's image as daring and different (in the turbulent times of 1999).

    Challenge: Keep one step ahead of an enthusiastic but critical *reformasi*-minded consumer.

- **Pond's Pore Strip (Philippines)**

    Objective: To launch a breakthrough blackhead-remover strip and establish it quickly before competitors could launch rival products.

    Challenge: Direct and control a trial among a notoriously fickle teen audience to prevent misuse (which makes the product ineffective).

How to locate a Challenge

The first thing to ask is: What's the block? Why are people not choosing the brand at all, or as often as we would like? What is the one big thing that is in the way of the brand achieving its objectives? Is the issue the brand or the category?

Answering these questions can reveal a diverse range of problems. For example:

- there are no distinctive icons (or there are ones that are seen as negative)
- there may be business practices which undermine claims that the brand is a good corporate citizen
- there is no strong image, or a bad/irrelevant image
- the product is outmoded or too niche
- the product is too dependent on core/transitional/repertoire buyers
- the product is seen in the wrong places (or not in the right places)
- the product is subject to buyers' conventional wisdom about when to buy or who to buy for.

Locating the block is fundamental to 360 Degree brand communications. It can be anything in the marketing mix, from a trade problem to a product design issue; from a consumer perception problem to a pricing problem; or even a category-relevance issue.

Six brand equities

The importance of the block is such that it is vital to isolate it upfront. In order to do so, it is perhaps easiest to channel one's thinking into the different areas in which the brand operates.

A brand can be said to have six areas of equity. Equity in each of these areas underpins brand equity as a whole:

1. **Product:** how the product performance supports the brand
2. **Image:** whether the brand's image is strong and engaging
3. **Customer:** how strong the brand's customer franchise is
4. **Channel:** how well the brand is leveraged in the trade environment
5. **Visual:** whether the brand presents a clear, consistent and differentiating presence
6. **Goodwill:** whether the brand is endorsed by influencers and the communities in which it lives

By thinking as a team about how the brand performs (or under-performs) in these areas, a key problem, issue or "block" will become apparent.

Here are some examples:

*   **Beer (Thailand)**
    People want something cheap (such as this beer) during a recession, but do not want to be seen as being cheap themselves.

*   **Coffee (China)**
    Coffee plays a minor role in Chinese lives: people see coffee as a transition marker in time (i.e. as a pre-dinner drink), rather than a transition marker in mood.

*   **Bird's Nest (Hong Kong)**
    Women think Bird's Nest is too precious (expensive) for personal use, so only buy it as a gift for special friends to help them have beautiful, glowing skin.

- **Online Broker (Hong Kong)**
  Having an account with a reputable broker stands the test of time — you feel your money is safe, even though you know they take some of the profit. Why risk safety by changing brokers?

Relevance

Initially, it often seems as if the brand has multiple blocks. In such cases, a common theme or thread will become evident that reveals the wider problem. Ultimately, a block is all about relevance of one form or another:

Consumer relevance ("That's not for people like me"; "I've never heard of it")

Price relevance ("It's not in my budget")

Category relevance ("It doesn't offer what I need")

Brand relevance ("My loyalty lies elsewhere")

Channel relevance ("It cannot be bought where I want to buy it")

Influence relevance ("It's not supported by the people I respect.")

Brand health check

A quick and easy way of assessing potential weaknesses is by way of a brand health check. By using a simple spider diagram (see Figure 4.1) to score a brand against each of the equities and comparing these scores with those of its competitors, areas of weakness will become visually apparent. Often, this is a good indication of where a block may lie.

From problems to solutions

Asking yourself how to overcome or get round the block is then the key to articulating a good Brand Challenge.

Figure 4.1 American Express vs Diners in Hong Kong

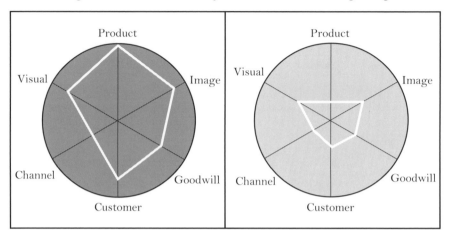

A good Brand Challenge is the creative springboard for all brand communications. It forms the guiding brief for all specialist disciplines to work from. It must inspire ideas and activities, but it should also provide a simple guide to whether they are the *right* ideas and activities. It might lead you to ask yourself whether a TV campaign will really help you to meet your Brand Challenge or whether PR is the obvious vehicle to change perceptions.

Everything springs from a Challenge. And so it needs to be positioned at the very heart of any agency's communication strategy brief (as indeed it is at Ogilvy).

From Challenge to Ideas

When articulating the Brand Challenge it is important to realize that we are part-way to the Idea. It is the big strategic breakthrough we have been waiting for.

Let's go back now to the examples of the blocks we mentioned earlier and see how this can be applied.

- **Beer (Thailand)**

  Block: People want something cheap (such as this beer) during a recession, but do not want to be seen as being cheap themselves.

  Challenge: Make people believe that with this beer they can turn every drinking occasion into party time.

- **Coffee (China)**

  Block: Coffee plays a minor role in Chinese lives: people see coffee as a transition marker in time (i.e. as a pre-dinner drink), rather than a transition marker in mood.

  Challenge: Get people to think of drinking coffee as a catalyst for stimulating conversations.

- **Bird's Nest (Hong Kong)**

  Block: Women think Bird's Nest is too precious (expensive) for personal use, so only buy it as a gift for special friends to help them have beautiful, glowing skin.

  Challenge: Make them feel that loving themselves is the most natural thing in the world — and that Bird's Nest should be a fundamental part of their own skincare regimen.

- **Online Broker (Hong Kong)**

  Block: Having an account with a reputable broker stands the test of time — you feel your money is safe, even though you know they take much of the profit. Why risk safety by changing brokers?

  Challenge: Shatter the assumption that all share-brokerage firms are designed to benefit brokers, not investors.

Remember: the key thing is to identify a singular Challenge. Never forget the dictum: *If all obstacles have to be overcome before you begin, nothing will ever be achieved.*

The following case study provides a clear example of what can be achieved by following this approach.

CASE STUDY 2

The Milo Challenge — reinvigorating an old favorite in Thailand

Background

Milo is an international brand with a powerful local identity which distinguishes it across almost two-thirds of the world's surface, on the Asian, African and Australasian continents.

From the start, it was positioned as an energy-and-health drink. Competition sports (including the Olympic Games as early as 1936) were used to communicate Milo's energy-giving benefit. Everywhere, it came to represent the quintessential sporting brand for children; whether they were young Filipinos playing basketball in the playground or Aussies surfing at the beach. And so, it became a powerful and valuable brand asset for Nestlé.

But, over time, two conditions have altered Milo's position. Firstly, in less developed Milo markets, diets have improved as the choice of alternative nutritional product sources became available, competing head on with Milo's core benefit. Secondly, the brand positioning, which has fundamentally not changed over the years, had become misinterpreted in many markets as being all about "winning at sport". This was particularly the case in Thailand.

Thailand is a challenger market where Milo is not number 1 in its category. Moreover, Thailand had not leveraged the true essence of the Milo brand and its sports association, as had been done in other markets.

Sport is a great unifier, as many brands have recognized, and can be a positive force which can forge new relationships and inspire and motivate kids and adults alike. Yes, its goal is to provide a winner — a clear, measurable outcome — but its spirit is one which uplifts the consciousness and provides moments of optimism, camaraderie and a "can do" attitude. Sport is a metaphor for winning in life ... providing lessons in sociability, confidence, reliability, discipline, grace, good humor and more. Sport is a metaphor for the hopes and dreams of kids.

While being associated with sport and winning had given Milo an enviable market positioning, it had become in need of redefinition. The focus on "winning at sport" was too narrow and too literal. Furthermore, this deep association with sport was not seen as relevant to the brand buyers in Thailand, the mothers — not always the biggest sports fans in the household.

The Block

The block to greater brand growth was seen to be in the relevance of a "winning at sports" positioning. The brand promise of helping kids to succeed needed to have a much wider interpretation than mere sporting prowess.

The Challenge

The key to Milo's revitalization and renewal lay in articulating the key Brand Challenge. Here was a highly successful brand: but to sustain future growth, it needed to evolve.

Many brands face simple (and large) problems and the challenges facing them are usually easy to identify (if harder to address!). Milo represented a trickier case, where identifying the Challenge would not be straightforward.

The objective set for the marketing department in Thailand was "To become the #1 tonic drink". However, the Challenge facing the brand in order to achieve that objective needed to be more focused. It had to make kids feel that Milo could help them fulfill their sporting dreams. The question, then, was: How to interpret "winning at sports" into a more meaningful concept?

Understanding the users

The core Milo users are kids aged between six and 12. At this age, they are on a voyage of discovery, living out their hopes and dreams and aspirations in the imaginative world of their daily lives. They enjoy pushing themselves in the effort to achieve the goal of the game.

The role of sports is to take time out from school, a time for friends and fun, not serious winning or success. It is a measure of physical energy and mental alertness, rather than mental determination; and a light lesson about life, teamwork and confidence.

Understanding the buyers

For mums, on the other hand, the role of sports is as a leisure activity for their kids; an outlet and release for fun, not a big aspiration; and a metaphor for energy and vitality.

Winning in sport is actually pretty far from a mother's mind. But in positioning terms, Milo was perceived to have a competitive attitude — to be pushing for victory at all times. This had become predictable, expected; predicating a relationship with the brand which was too prescriptive and, for many, too intense.

A new Brand Challenge

The Challenge facing Ogilvy was to rewrite some of the rules about Milo — to widen the scope for brand messages and to reframe this whole discussion about "winning".

The key to unlocking the Brand Challenge was to acknowledge that, actually, the important thing in sport isn't *winning*, but having the energy to be your best in the game (or, from Mum's perspective, read "game of life").

In short, Milo needed to own the *energy to succeed*.

The Work

- **Milo sports camps**:
  Milo has become a major sponsor of school sports and coaching activities. And by engaging some of each nation's best players in these training

Milo's support of grassroots sports

50

camps, it has provided kids with an inspiration to really perform at their best — a value that is dear to the heart of any parent.

- In Thailand, programs were organized in conjunction with the Ministry of Education. These were extended through "Improve your skills" wall charts, and a series of quarter marathons that were aimed at uncovering new talent in rural areas. Through its sponsorship of a weekly children's TV program — *Noo Tham Dai* ("Kids, you can do it!") — Milo became the sole sponsor of Sports Star Search, which underpinned the program of the company's school visits, activities and sports camps.

- This thinking was taken ever deeper in Malaysia, already one of Milo's strongest markets. Milo's activities included national promotions which have become part of the national cultural consciousness. To raise support for the national athletes at the Asean Games, Milo organized a mass collection of signatures, kicked-off by the Minister for Sport. A huge canvas was transported around the country for people to sign as part of other Milo events. This raised awareness of the Games, as well as keeping Milo in the forefront of people's minds. Millions of supporters' signatures were captured. It is not surprising that the national chant which accompanies these types of activities — *Malaysia Boleh* (Malaysia can!) — is now synonymous with the Milo brand.

The ongoing situation

Milo is a brand that demands that we constantly update and explore positive sporting links in everything that we do especially in a "Challenger Market" like Thailand. At the core of all this is a clear understanding of what makes the brand resonate: Milo is not a selfish brand, but rather one that offers optimism to all around. It helps fuel the hopes, imagination and aspirations of young children everywhere, and offers the promise of a good life for them to their mums.

"i-Mode" in Japan

In Japan, the future is already happening and its name is "i-mode".

One of the most successful technologies ever developed, i-mode is the world's first mobile Internet technology. Since its introduction in February 1999, it has amassed an incredible 32 million subscribers, making it the fastest-adopted technology ever. Some 37.5% of the population aged between 15 and 65 are subscribers, and the list increases by 28,000 new subscribers each day.

Thus, i-mode users represent a broad cross-section of Japanese society and include young, middle-aged and old people (the heaviest users are actually women in their late 20s). Almost all subscribers are active users: most of them use e-mail or browse web pages from their hand-phones every single day. Simply put, i-mode has revolutionized the way more than one-third of Japanese people live and work, and has redefined mobile communications.

The inventor of i-mode is said to be Mari Matsunaga of the Japanese telecommunications giant NTT-DoCoMo (in Japanese, *doco mo* means "anyplace you go" and the acronym is used to stand for **Do C**ommunication **O**ver the **Mo**bile Network). The profitability of the business model has turned many NTT-DoCoMo shareholders into US$-millionaires overnight. Its market value (capitalization) makes it one of the highest valued companies in the world.

What exactly is it? Essentially, i-mode works in the same way as the fixed Internet. A browser in the i-mode handset allows the user to view i-mode-enabled sites. Simply pushing the i-mode button on the handset calls up the i-mode portal's main menu, which in turn gives access to the "certified" content. The user can also enter a URL to view "independent" (non-certified) compatible sites directly.

How does it work? Technically, i-mode is an overlay on NTT-DoCoMo's ordinary mobile voice system. While the voice system is "circuit-switched" (i.e. you need to dial up), i-mode is "packet-switched". This means that i-mode is, in principle, "always on", provided you are in an area where the signal can reach you. When you select an i-mode item on the handset menu, the data is usually downloaded immediately.

Typically, users send e-mail, look at the weather forecast, look at sports results, load ringing melodies into their handsets, play games, do online banking and stock trading, purchase air and train tickets, download cartoons and images, look for restaurants and look for new friends. Increasingly, corporations are also using i-mode for internal work, such as supply-chain management.

Of course, it is also a powerful marketing communications medium. In one of the more sophisticated uses of i-mode for brand communications purposes, Nestlé developed a recipe-based site. By tracking the daily hit rates, they were able to tell the precise times that users were logging-on to look up recipes. They were then able to develop and deploy *time-sensitive* e-mail and SMS advertising to alert potential users to the recipe site. Not surprisingly, this was when people were on their way home, and thinking about what to have for dinner! i-mode uses cHTML (compact HTML), which is a subset of ordinary HTML. In addition, there are special DoCoMo characters (image characters called *emoji*), which are symbols for joy, kisses, love, sadness, hot-spring baths, telephone, Shinkansen train, encircled numbers etc. There are quite a large number of these special non-standardized characters, and DoCoMo adds new image characters from time to time.

There is no one single reason why i-mode is so successful. Certainly, a considerable factor in this was the fact that NTT-DoCoMo made it easy for developers to develop websites, so that content was never going to be a problem. But other contributory factors include:

- the fact that PCs in Japanese homes are not as widespread as in the U.S. and Europe (meaning that Japanese people don't use PCs for Internet access as much)
- the relatively low price of i-mode-enabled handsets meant a low entrance threshold
- high mobile phone penetration (60 million mobile subscribers)
- a general love of gadgets amongst the Japanese people
- the fact that i-mode is always on (within signal range)
- charges that are geared to information accessed rather than usage time, resulting in relatively low fees
- an efficient billing system via the mobile phone bill
- the fact that i-mode achieved fashion status
- an effective and efficient marketing campaign
- the fact that it uses cHTML, which makes it easy for both developers and ordinary consumers to develop content (which assured an explosive growth in every sort of content).

But the one "killer app" was e-mail. By allowing users to send and receive e-mail from anywhere (especially a commuter train), it assured its own success, just as e-mail helped spread Internet growth in the initial years.

One of the lasting conundrums about i-mode concerns the question "What does the 'i' stand for?". In the broader sense, it means as much as the "k" in Kodak. There is no single meaning to the "i". In the Japanese language there are literally hundreds of words pronounced "i", one of which means "love" (and this has been successfully exploited in some of DoCoMo's advertising campaigns). But the advice is not to spend too much time thinking about what the "i" means. In fact, it might be more useful to see the "i" not as a letter, but as a graphical element — in Japan, it is common practice to use English words for graphical effect without worrying too much about what those words actually mean!

i-mode is currently arriving in a small way in Europe from April 2002 (in Germany and the Netherlands), and we can expect to see a substantial uptake over the next few years. After all, 32 million people can't be wrong.

Northwest Airlines Treasure Hunt

▼TRANSLATION

Treasure Hunt USA

Take the quiz and you could go to the USA

Its free to play.

Todays Prize
Narita / San Francisco
Travel ticket

1. Play
2. Ranking
3. Winners List
4. Instruction
5. Registration

▼TRANSLATION

Question 29
What do you call the bag that lets you take home food you haven't finished in a restaurant in the US?

1. Kitty Bag
2. Happy Bag
3. Biggy Bag
4. Doggy Bag

Orientating Around a Brand Challenge

Northwest Airlines Treasure Hunt

Congratulations!!

You've succeeded in
the treasure hunt to
the state of Alaska.

You get a chance to win
today's prize.

Miles won:
+10 Miles
Total Miles:
141 Miles

Northwest Airlines Treasure Hunt

Akira

Total Miles
225 Miles

Ranking
131st out of 19,345 Players

Maximum Miles to date
290 Miles

The highly successful Northwest Airlines i-mode Treasure Hunt.
(Reproduced with kind permission of Northwest Airlines)

5

What Makes a Great Brand Idea?

"I do not seek. I find."
Pablo Picasso

Tham Khai Meng, the Regional Creative Director of Ogilvy & Mather Asia-Pacific, calls ideas the "Trojan Horses" of the communications business, allowing a brand to "get under the defenses" of consumers.

It is a nice analogy. Ideas can seem simple, innocuous things but they have immense significance when it comes to brand warfare.

In the 360 Degree Brand Stewardship[SM] context, an idea is a bridge between the shared experiences, feelings and associations of different individuals. The idea is part of the brand's DNA, and should meet the Challenge facing the brand.

It is the role of *everyone* in the agency to understand, sell, evaluate and talk about ideas — constantly. As David Ogilvy has pointed out, "Senior men have no monopoly on great ideas. Nor do creative people. Some of the best ideas come from account executives, researchers and others. Encourage this; you need all the ideas you can get."

What is "an idea"?

But, despite their obvious importance, the subject of exactly what ideas are and how they work is avoided by most commentators in business.

The reason for this may have something to do with the fact that it is remarkably difficult to define an "idea". A dictionary is not particularly helpful in this respect either, listing among its definitions "mental concept or image"; "opinion or belief"; "plan, scheme"; "vague impression (with meaning or significance)" and "a model by which all real things are but imperfect imitations (Plato)".

None of these explanations is very useful for us. A better, classic definition comes from Arthur Koestler: "An idea is a bi-sociation of two or more previously unconnected thought matrices."

A simpler version of the same thought comes from James Webb Young, the creative director of J. Walter Thompson (JWT) in the 1920s: "An idea is nothing more nor less than a new combination of old elements."

Even these are not very easy to comprehend. Are ideas so commonplace that perhaps they defy definition?

Idea generation

The commonplace is actually a good place to start. Imagine you wake up on a Saturday morning and the diary is empty. You have nothing planned for the weekend (it can happen!). A lazy lie-in followed by a slow breakfast may while away a few hours. But, at some point, you have got to *do* something. What do you do?

You *think*. "What am I going to do?" is a thought process. A number of different thoughts run through your head: go shopping ... to the cinema ... to a restaurant ... to a bar; meet friends; read a book; whatever. You engage in the process of selecting an activity.

For each selected activity in turn, you think (perhaps

58

subconsciously): "What is it going to do *for me*?" This is the emotional context, and is all about feelings you get from doing certain activities: excitement, self-indulgence, intellectual stimulation, chilling out, keeping up ... with fashion, gossip, events etc.

Finally, you decide to read a *certain* book, go to a *particular* film, see a *special* friend, visit a *specific* restaurant. Your choice reflects the emotional needs you have on that day.

Deconstructing such choices is an almost impossible task, because there are so many variables at play. These include:

- situational (what you did last weekend, what your friends have done recently, what is easily available, the weather)
- personality (what your hobbies are, whether you are more introspective or extrovert, your values)
- psychological (what emotional reward you are looking for, the end benefit you want).

The list goes on. Often, you may not understand why you made the choice you made. It is an instinctive thing, which just somehow fits your mood and offers the right kind of stimulation, and *involves* you in some way.

So, the process of idea-generation and selection is one of combining:

- conscious reasoning ("What shall I *do*?")
- emotional evaluation ("What will this do *for me*?")
- instinctive decision-making ("What is the ideal stimulus for me *right now*?").

So, putting this with our previous definitions, an idea could be defined as:

"An unexpected combination of different thoughts which puts 'something' in a new and involving context."

In the business of brand communications, this "something" is the brand. Just as deciding what to do at the weekend combines conscious reasoning with emotional evaluation with instinctive decision-making, so it is with developing brand ideas.

Typically, we consider the key *situational* variables of the brand's current performance and image, the target consumer and how he or she thinks, feels and acts, and the competitive environment of what rival brands are doing and what is happening in the media and marketplace.

It is when we get to the *personality* and *psychological* variables that we often get into trouble in business. This is because people tend to have a natural assumption that everyone thinks just as they do. Well, they don't. Everyone has their own thoughts and expectations of an idea in the business of brand-building. Each is partly right, and therefore partly wrong.

Different perspectives

At the simplest level, there are *three* basic perspectives to be aware of: at the two extremes there are clients and creative people, while account management and planning people sit somewhere in between. They each have a different perspective because they each have different roles to play.

Clients want to build their business, so they tend to see ideas as things that help crystallize a strategic positioning that they can use to *define* the essence of what the brand does. Sometimes, these are called "positioning ideas", "organizing ideas" or "vision ideas". They come from the perspective of the company, its business relationships and the need to create a coherent and consistent understanding of the brand and its role in the business. In marketing textbooks, this is often called the "push" approach.

Account and Planning people in agencies look for a creative breakthrough that *redefines* the way people see the brand through the vehicle of a specific concept or image. This is sometimes called the "brand idea" or "selling idea" or "advertising idea". Their perspective is driven by insights into what they think is most likely to inform, inspire and motivate the consumer. Business schools call this the "pull" approach.

Creative people (art directors, copywriters, photographers, film directors, editors) look for visual and verbal devices that help *refine* (i.e. enhance) the image people have of the brand. Their objective is to find things that will stimulate people to link their own experiences or expectations with the brand benefit. These are called "creative ideas" or "executional ideas" and are brought alive through the use of "techniques". This is where the hardest and most detailed work goes on in an agency. A particular image, a turn of phrase, a camera angle, the use of color and layout can all have a major impact on the success of an executional idea in the marketplace.

All three have to be synchronized in order for an idea to have a powerful impact on the market.

Breakthrough ideas

For an idea to assume the status of an "involving" or "breakthrough" idea it has to surprise people in some way. We call this "making the familiar strange, and the strange familiar". Think about it. How do you make something that people know very well (tissue paper, perhaps, or a pint of beer) seem different? Or how do you make something that people are totally unfamiliar with (a new type of food, perhaps) seem part of everyday life, when their natural instinct would be to avoid it like the plague? And, if you succeed, think about how involving the impression you make will be.

Take, for example, the standard in-flight safety announcement on board an aircraft before takeoff — something we have all heard a dozen times before. In fact, we are so familiar with it, we rarely hear the words. We probably pretend to listen while, instead, we flick through a magazine. How to take something so familiar and make it seem different enough to get people's attention? Try the official Southwest Airlines safety announcement: "There may be 50 ways to leave your lover, but

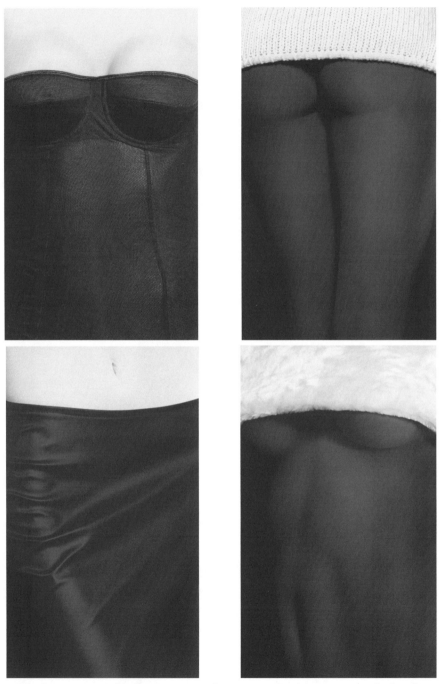

What's on your mind? Guinness — a classic example of how to make the familiar seem strange
(Reproduced with kind permission of Gaelic Inns)

there are only six exits from this aircraft. We suggest you note their position now."

Let's look again at the Trojan Horse. In the siege of Troy, the ancient Greeks were unable to win the battle through traditional warfare. So they built a huge wooden horse and left it outside the gates of the city, ostensibly as a gift for the people of Troy. The wooden horse was wheeled inside the city gates by the citizens of Troy. At dead of night, out slipped some Greek soldiers who had been hiding inside, overpowered the guards, and opened the gates to let the Greek army swarm in and take the city.

A nice story. But also a breakthrough idea. The Greeks were looking for people on the inside who could open the gates. The normal thinking process in such a situation includes placing spies and cultivating traitors inside the enemy's camp. However, even if this had been possible, they would not have had the weaponry

Fish-flavored ice-cream from Japan — making the strange seem familiar

to overpower armed guards. In this case, spies and traitors are not big ideas.

What made the Trojan Horse a big, breakthrough idea was that it combined two previously unconnected things: a nice gift and a nasty surprise. It was through this combination that the idea took the people of Troy unawares. (The Trojan Horse was a *strange* device in an act of war, but a *familiar* tactic of sneaking behind the defenses of the enemy.)

Breakthrough ideas (rather than just conventional "thoughts") always combine two previously unconnected things. And they do it in a way that surprises us. They give us new perspectives on our world. We change our beliefs, values or actions as a result of these ideas. We are involved, and we admire the creator of the idea — whether a religious leader, a military commander, an artist, philosopher, or (let's face it) a Cannes-winning advertising creative director.

Three levels of idea

An idea is really composed of three distinct levels:

- The Strategic Idea (this defines the essence of what we are trying to achieve — the Challenge)
- The Brand Idea (this redefines the way we "see" the Challenge by providing a specific concept/image)
- The Executional Idea (this refines the image in a way that enables us to project our own experiences/expectations onto the brand).

Let's take Marlboro cigarettes to illustrate this. The Marlboro brand could be defined in the following terms:

Strategic Idea: *A cigarette that celebrates real men and their desire for freedom* (based on the insight that real men believe that "Man was born free and real men stay that way!")

Brand Idea: *Use the "Wild West" as a symbol for self-discovery, adventure and the proof of masculinity*

64

Executional Idea: *The Marlboro cowboy alone on the plains of America.*

Christmas card received by author from the Leo Burnett agency in 1996

Or we could take IBM's repositioning exercise, which was started in 1994, as another example.

IBM is a classic example of a big brand that was in trouble in the early 1990s, against a backdrop of US$18-billion-losses over three years. Sales were declining and the brand was seen as arrogant and out of date. Compared to the nimble, aggressive new players in the computing market, such as Compaq, Acer and Microsoft, IBM was seen as sluggish, even timid.

The company was served by hundreds of different communications suppliers, so there was no consistency to its branding efforts; and it was even considering breaking up into a dozen or more "little blues".

However, with the help of 360 Degree Brand Stewardship[SM], IBM was able to turn its biggest liability — its size — into its greatest asset by *redefining* what it stood for. The IBM brand idea — that *only* IBM could provide "solutions for a small planet" —

was built on the fact that *only* IBM was large enough, broad-ranging enough and brave enough to brand the concept of "the global village". This was a concept that had previously terrified most people. IBM made it seem benign and charming.

It was an idea that was able to unite the many parts of the IBM business, and give them a sense of direction and ownership of the brand that had not been so clearly felt or articulated before. It was an idea that gave back to IBM its confidence. It was an idea that gave it back its brand: one brand, one voice.

It is also an idea that positions IBM as the brand owner of the rich, fertile and exploding world of e-business. And it is an idea that helped make customers across the world feel a tremendous empathy with IBM.

So, how can we define the idea in its constituent parts?

Strategic Idea: *Bring a human dimension to technology and its role in creating the "global village"*

Brand Idea: *Solutions for a small planet*

Executional Idea: *Unexpected users, everywhere, are enfranchised through technology*

You may remember some of the famous advertising ideas which brought this to life, from monks in Thailand using their ThinkPads to e-mail, to the Pope in the Vatican, to nomads navigating across the Sahara desert with the help of IBM technology.

A good idea can be taken anywhere ...

Do you remember Deep Blue™, the super-computer that defeated Gary Kasparov at chess? Even though there is no symbol, no computer, no logo, no headline or copy even to hint at any brand in this picture, most people remember IBM. How is this so? Because IBM and its communications partners (including O&M) made it happen by understanding the Brand Idea and what it means in the hearts of consumers.

Gary Kasporov vs IBM Deep Blue™

Strategic vs executional ideas

This three-stage description of an idea should not be confused as a process. There is not necessarily a linear progression from one to the next. Great ideas are often executional first, and only then become expressed as creative and strategic ideas. As John Locke said, "The connecting is the thinking". We often think in terms of pictures, but by expressing the idea as a strategic or creative concept, we are able to preserve it, and can facilitate further executions in the same vein, without milking an executional device to death.

Ideas are often produced through a seemingly random series of cause and effect (like a pattern that emerges gradually). But, this actually belies a quite rigorous and focused intention on the part of the brand owner to achieve a consistent message.

Different types of breakthrough idea

There are many ways brands achieve that elusive goal of making a breakthrough impact.

- **Brand Missions**

  There are brands that wear their hearts on their sleeves. These brands clearly define what their purpose in life is. Consider the following examples:

  IBM   : Make the global village a reality

  Apple   : Democratize technology

  BP   : Make energy respect human progress

  Virgin   : Challenge monopolies

  Sony   : Champion innovation

  Pepsi   : Celebrate each "new generation"

  Milo   : Fulfill kids' sporting dreams

  Benetton : Highlight prejudice wherever it exists

- **Core Attitudes/Values**

  These brands stand for some integral value, and ensure that all activities reflect this attitude:

  VW   : Total reliability

  Nike   : Irreverence justified

  Pond's   : A haven of trust in a hyped-up world

  Guinness : Strength, virility and substance

- **Benefits**

  These brands identify a core generic virtue of the category, and make it seem like the only benefit you need:

  Coke   : Refreshment within an arm's reach of desire

  Dove   : Femininity restored

  Patek Philippe : A contemporary heirloom

- **User Imagery**

  Some brands identify with the inner psychological drivers or beliefs of their consumers:

  Levi's   : Teenage independence and rebellion

  Marlboro   : Man was born free, and real men stay that way

  Johnnie Walker : The confidence to be yourself, whatever

Nine secrets about having great ideas

If having ideas is an obligation for anyone working to create powerful and effective 360 Degree brands, then ideas about "how to have Ideas" may be welcome. We don't claim to be able to bestow the gift of inspiration on anyone, but here are nine things we have learnt along the way about having Ideas. We hope they might be of some value to you:

1. **Out with the abstract**

   Defining the characteristics of great Ideas in the abstract will not help you create one in the slightest. You need to get your hands dirty. You need to try an idea out, size it up, put it on, knock it about a bit, see what it looks like with its clothes off, or upside down, or against the skyline. Only by having lots of ideas will you ever get to a good one.

2. **Emotional mothering**

   Some people are supposed to be better than others at having ideas. We call them "creative teams" and they tend to be sensitive types.

   The best ideas come out of a process of "emotional mothering" of the creative team. The big leap in the whole 360 Degree process is unearthing executional ideas.

   Stimulation to achieve this comes in all forms and sizes: an object, an analogy, a proverb, a joke. Make the team feel good about their ideas. Let them down gently. Encourage them frequently. Inspire them. Remember there is a difference between the brief (which provides information and insight) and the briefing (to provide inspiration and brand experience).

   But do not forget that some of the best ideas never came from a creative department. Good ideas can come from anywhere. It is the obligation of everyone to be an "ideas originator" in a 360 Degree world.

3. **The blind creator**

The creator of the big idea sometimes fails to recognize it as such. That's why we need to work together. It takes insight and understanding to spot the big idea lying in a mountain of rubbish. Raw ideas need to be worked and reworked.

Often it is the Account Planner's role to articulate, shape, mould, edit, thin-out and bring to the fore the big, simple, clean and pure Brand Idea. Thus, when presented with an idea, it is important to look behind the detail, and try to see and articulate the bigger, macro idea lurking within. It is the articulation of the underlying idea that allows its dramatization in many different guises in many different media.

The Idea should be elegantly expressed, in order to be universally understood: precisely defined, neat, simple, balanced, and offered to the world in an expression that "feels right".

4. **Mind the gaps**

There are hundreds of stages during which good ideas can be lost, from the brief-writing to the brainstorming to the evaluation to the presentation and the research.

There are plenty of opportunities to kill a good idea. Making the logo bigger, adding more detail, selling harder, to a wider and wider target — all represent clutter which weakens ideas like a virus. Get the wrong visual aids, the wrong presenter, the wrong set of words describing the idea, the wrong researcher, the wrong respondent, and your idea is still-born and you can kiss it goodbye.

Beware of selling your idea through a chain of command. Everyone has their own point of view which they add (helpfully, they think) to an idea. Few people want to subtract from an idea, yet this can often be the best way to preserve its integrity.

HOW TO CARVE
AN
ELEPHANT

There was once, in India, an old woodcarver who was famous for carving elephants.
Other people carve elephants, too, of course, but the old man's elephants were, somehow, more galumphing
and trumpety. One day, a documentary film-crew was sent to interview him.
"What do you do," he was asked," to make your elephants so perfect?" This was his reply:

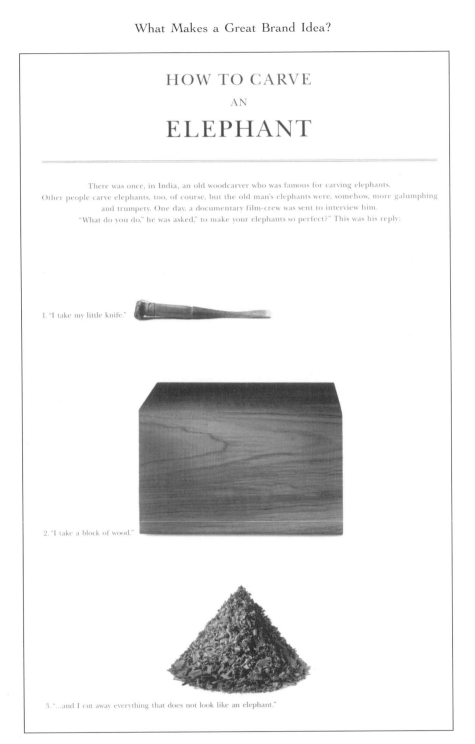

1. "I take my little knife."

2. "I take a block of wood."

3. "...and I cut away everything that does not look like an elephant."

The "Art of Craft" by Ogilvy's Worldwide Creative Director, Neil French
(Reproduced with kind permission of Ogilvy & Mather)

Ideas need protecting and nurturing. There are a million reasons to kill a great idea. And only one reason to pursue it — namely, that great ideas make great brands.

5. Everything is relative

Clients assess ideas *relatively*, not absolutely. Actually, it is next to impossible to assess an idea "absolutely" — there is no global, standard, quantifiable scale of quality when it comes to ideas. Ideas are ephemeral, qualitative, subjective. Anyone trying to judge the quality of an idea, and whether it will be right for their brand, will assess it against other ideas. These may be others they see in a presentation, others they have seen before, what their competitors are doing, what a favorite or admired brand is up to.

Perhaps using the following simple technique to help you evaluate an idea might help you sell it to a client, by doing the relative contrasting *for* the client (as long as you are sure you have a good idea to hand!). It is called the CLIMB technique and answers some vital questions :

C   How well does it **C**ommunicate what we are looking for?
L   What makes it **L**ikeable?
I   Why will it generate **I**mpact?
M   In what way is it **M**otivating?
B   Is it well **B**randed (or something that a brand could own)?

6. Research can be murderous

Research can kill your best ideas. But it can also save them. That is why having some of your organization's best brains looking after the research at every stage is vital. Everything from stimulus to moderator to respondent recruitment to observation and analysis needs to be overseen to make sure it is sensitive to the brand's needs, and that the idea gets a fair showing.

Similarly, research evidence can be invaluable in saving an idea from the scrap heap. Clients like evidence and data. Often, this can be instrumental in getting an idea to the next level.

7. Know the difference

The best creative ideas can become strategic ideas, as much as vice versa. The creative line may well be the best articulation of a strategic idea. Similarly, the strategic concept may well be impossible to better. As long as the idea is right for the brand and meets the challenge, then it's a good one.

It is also important to know where the similarities stop and the differences begin — each culture has unique traditions of style, spirit and conventions. For example, humor crosses borders, but comedians often don't. Each target audience has different needs and expectations. So while the strategic and creative ideas are consistent, the executional ideas can vary.

8. Demonstrate your passion

Recognize that, at all times and in all places, *all* of our jobs are about ideas — developing them, understanding them, building on them, selling them, talking about them and *living* them. Passion and ideas are inextricable.

9. Do not fear the irrational

Great ideas are seldom completely rational. In Daniel Goldman's book *Emotional Intelligence*, he begins to explain why the irrational, the intangible and the unquantifiable are so powerful:

> *"The* amygdala, *the oldest part of the human brain, is almost fully formed at birth. It is the passion centre of our brains and it's here where we learn the survival skills, the love skills, the bonding skills and the understanding skills. This is the reason*

why it is believed that the first four years of a human's life are the most important, because it is the amygdala *which forms the foundation of our being. It is only after this that we begin to learn rational things."*

All great ideas have a large dose of the intangible and the unquantifiable. Don't waste time trying to demystify an idea; rather, embrace its very irrationality.

And finally...

Always remember David Ogilvy's famous dictum: *"Unless your advertising is built on a Big Idea, it will pass like a ship in the night."*

The following case study provides an example of how a great idea can be made bigger and better by the process of taking it through more and more media, reaching into consumers' lives in new and different ways.

CASE STUDY 3

San Miguel Light Beer (HK)
"We are all now working for Sammy."
Mike Wong, Managing Director, Ogilvy & Mather, Hong Kong

Background

Even as Hong Kong's leading local beer brand, San Miguel was not immune to decline. Having weathered a tough period, by the end of 2000 the brand had successfully revitalized its brand image in a highly competitive market where imports were seen as more aspirational. Market share was stabilized and the bonding with the core drinker group, the 35-plus consumers, was consolidated.

This success, however, begged the next question: how to bond with the younger drinker who is both the evangelist and the future core consumer? The need to extend the reach of the San Miguel portfolio was all the more important in the face of a shrinking beer category, with alternative beverage choices — trendy green tea, bottled water, and even milk — being seen as cooler.

The offer of a lighter-tasting beer would be fresh news; but a launch as important as this required a big brand idea. Relevance was vital. The question was how to create the most relevant vehicle to tap into this untouched segment — a vibrant target group who were young, more active and lived a slightly more health-conscious lifestyle.

Understanding the young "soft drink" graduates

We spent a great deal of time and effort looking closely at the beer market, the products available and the target itself to ascertain what might bring the brand closer to a notoriously fickle and hard-to-reach consumer. We looked and listened to this group for a considerable period of time — in focus groups, by eavesdropping on them while hanging out on the streets, sidling up to them in retail outlets, photo-documenting their lives. We also talked to experts like university professors and social workers who studied this youth sector.

We were especially concerned about the paradox of a "light beer". "Light" has good connotations because it's low in alcohol, low in calories, a little bit more healthy. But it's also seen as being for nerds — boring, decidedly un-cool and bland. So … a tricky one … how to position a light beer and remain relevant to this small but influential crowd. A big idea was critical.

We also had to factor in that this was a line extension, not a new brand. We had to tie in with the flagship brand. If San Miguel (the parent brand) was "interesting and enjoyable", then San Miguel Light needed to be doubly so. If San Miguel was "fresh", then San Miguel Light needed to be fresher. But what does "interesting and fresh" mean to this particular target group?

"Free-floating in a world of illogical logic"

Our research began to tell us that this was a very strange world they inhabited. This group likes nothing better than to hang out and talk, but the talk is disorganized and chaotic. Discontinuous, shifting and bordering on the random, their logic and language are very different from ours!

They are easily bored and home is the most boring place of all. So they are driven out — out into the metropolis of urban Hong Kong. But when they get out, they don't always have a clear purpose — they want to "find fun", but it's an aimless objective, driven simply by the company of friends.

Instant gratification is everything. They are crazy for visual and sensory stimuli, anything that hints of mischief-making, that is visually fun; but, like the images from comics, everything is instantly disposable and it's on to find the next "hit".

They are aimless, but they are, in a way that only they can be, also very connected.

Defining the Brand Challenge … Enter Sammy

The Brand Challenge was to make San Miguel Light the "mischief-maker" that surrounds the aimless, listless, empty-but-connected lives of the young "soft drink" graduates.

To meet this Challenge, we invented Sammy.

The Brand Idea

Here's Sammy.

Forget about whether you like the ads or not; the truth is, Sammy is in all of us. He's the naughty, but largely harmless, little devil hidden within our personality. We all think about him but seldom have the courage to let him have his way. Nobody will hate Sammy because they will recognize that he is part of us. So we can laugh at him; he is the class joker, the ultimate spontaneous animal.

He is a boy, and he loves girls; so most of his jesting is aimed at women. But don't worry, he treats everyone equally … badly.

Populating Sammy's world

With an idea as big and unstoppable as Sammy, our job simply became one of finding a world for him to inhabit, where Sammy the naughty little prankster could come to life.

We simply needed to put Sammy in front of the public and let him do the rest. So, we gave him a TV schedule, let him parade up and down outdoors, let him sneak into karaoke clubs and haunt drinking dens. We printed him, made him viral, put him online and allowed him out at events.

The Results

Sammy was definitely the talk of the town. He got major publicity coverage and inspired provocative debate on his moral implications — was it right or wrong to appeal to baser instincts? The response in chat-room talk was one of wild excitement and hilarious exclamations. We had created a cool "idea" overnight.

Across Hong Kong, awareness rocketed in less than three weeks of the brand's introduction. The "advertising awareness" level amongst the target 18–24-year-olds was as high as 98%, while the "aided brand awareness" was 94%.

For the online connection with the target, there was massive click-through on the online advertisement — 31.9% in hongkong.com compared to the industry norm of 0.5%.

And they were thrilled by the viral touch-points — there were massive download levels for Sammy's screensaver and cursor.

On the business front, 68% of the entire annual sales target was achieved within four months, and this despite unforeseen restrictions on distribution. For the full year, even the revised targets were exceeded. We could look back at the accomplishment — we had a strong brand established firmly amongst the young drinkers. The strength of Sammy is still growing through viral efforts. The market even responded with its own version of Sammy handbags on sale in the world's busiest shopping district, Causeway Bay.

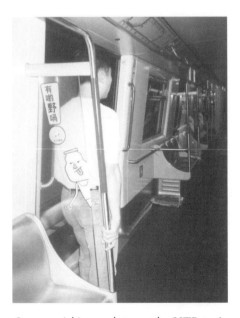

Sammy picking pockets on the MTR train

Sammy showing his better side on beer mats

Sammy's view on romance

Sammy's perspective of women
(Reproduced with kind permission of San Miguel)

Wells And Hand-pumps: A Rural Marketing Campaign In India

In India, 40% of the country's population fall into a category termed "media dark". These are the rural inhabitants, who fall outside the reach of mainstream media such as TV, newspapers, outdoor posters or commercial radio. Yet they are also brand buyers, and manufacturers need to find alternative ways of increasing awareness and communicating their product's point of difference to these people.

Unilever's Personal and Fabric wash division is one of these manufacturers. It suffered from low brand awareness, low trial, and a lack of saliency (top-of-mind awareness). The division approached Outreach (part of the Ogilvy Group), a company specializing in rural marketing (and which has an implementation workforce of over 50,000 people on tap), who identified a unique media-set: sources of water. Here was the ultimate point of brand–consumer interaction, and the most appropriate media for the job in hand — to raise top-of-mind awareness when consumers are at their most receptive.

Stickers were placed on water pumps, tiles cemented onto wells, tinplates pinned to trees and demonstrations organized for the weekly village markets (because in India, seeing is believing).

The scale of the operation was massive: 7,000 live demonstration shows were put on; 14,000 wells were painted; 63,000 hand-pumps were "stickered"; 23,000 tiles were fixed to wells; and 10,000 "implementers" were paid to help out.

All of which goes to show that effective brand communications need not be limited by a lack of "conventional" media. Media is infinite.

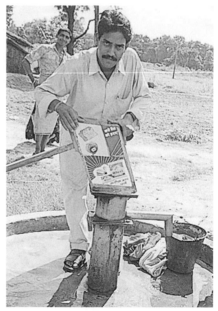

A typical well in rural India

6

Brand Loyalty is The Ultimate Goal

"True loyalty cannot be bought; it needs to be inspired."
British Army Officer Training Manual

A short detour

Having established some of the main tenets of 360 Degree brand building, we would now like to take a step back and look at the wider issue of what the ultimate goal of developing a brand in this way might be. As the subtitle to this book indicates, we firmly believe that a 360 Degree brand will be far more effective than a two-dimensional one. The reasons that underpin this claim are based on the effects 360 Degree Branding® has on brand loyalty. Brand loyalty is a fascinating concept because it has two wonderfully incongruous aspects to it. On the one hand, brand loyalty is an *emotional* commitment from a customer to a brand, and as such it is hard to describe and difficult to pin down. On the other hand, it involves a precise and *rational* science in measuring both loyalty itself and the financial benefits it can achieve.

And so this chapter takes a short detour from the process of "how to build 360 Degree brands" to look at the components and mechanics of customer loyalty. It is our belief that creating sustainable brand loyalty is the key commercial rationale for investing in the development of a 360 Degree brand. And perhaps it is therefore no coincidence that this is the middle chapter of the book: like the hub of a wheel or the fulcrum of a compass, the 360 Degree brand revolves around a comprehensive understanding of how brand loyalty is created and quantified.

The "CRM" phenomenon

Talk about "loyalty" has reached fever pitch in the last few years. This has been fueled by the growth of a new marketing industry, CRM — customer-relationship management. CRM is becoming *the* buzz-phrase of the new millennium. Everyone is using it. Everyone believes they need it. Because it promises to deliver "customer loyalty" on a new scale. To give some idea of its popularity, CRM investments are set to increase from US$11 billion to US$36 billion by 2004. Depending on the business they are in, *each* of the 3,500 companies that operate globally will invest between US$50 million and US$130 million in CRM over the next three years. (*Source*: QCI)

And yet, despite all these investments, a recent Ogilvy study showed that 70% of all CRM programs turn out to be flops. Why is this? We believe that this sorry state of affairs can only be the result of a fundamental misunderstanding of the relationship between CRM and brand loyalty, and, therefore, what CRM is capable of delivering to the brand.

The issue lies in the difference between the rational processes recommended by most implementers of CRM programs, and the emotional loyalty which gives any brand its true strength. At worst, CRM is seen as a piece of software, which will magically enable your business to achieve, enhance and deepen the relationship between you and your customer, while at the same time reducing the cost of each individual interaction. Normally the cost saving is achieved by removing the human element from many of the transactions, particularly for those customers who are not seen as particularly valuable. However loyalty is deepest when nurtured through a real relationship — difficult to achieve through an automated call center.

CRM is also expected to provide you with one holistic view of the customer, integrating all the relationships they may have had, or want to have — no matter which channel they come through. This provides a deeper knowledge of their real needs and value, and enables a better level of understanding, leading to deeper loyalty. It sounds great in theory, but is exceptionally difficult to achieve — and when it goes wrong, it strikes a jarring note with the customer.

Therefore, we believe that although loyalty is undoubtedly key to building a 360 Degree brand, it will only be achieved by understanding how loyalty works, and can be created, from the customer's perspective.

What is loyalty?

Under a layman's definition, loyalty is a noble quality. It involves unquestioning allegiance to a leader, a flag or a cause, or the peer group, *despite* adverse conditions or temptation from elsewhere. To stand by your leader/flag/group through trouble demonstrates loyalty, and reveals its noble qualities.

In marketing, the definition is equally clear, if a little less noble. There are two oft-repeated maxims:

- 20% of your customers account for 80% of your business
- it is five- to seven-times more profitable to sell to an existing customer than a new one.

Rather less well-known, but equally important, is the fact that it can cost more than seven-times as much to re-acquire a lapsed customer as it did to acquire them in the first place. So, customer loyalty means nothing less than business success. It costs a lot less to keep a loyal customer than to recruit a new one. Loyal customers keep coming back for more, time and time again, and sustain your business at a profitable transaction margin. What is more, they spend more per visit than irregular customers. And what's even better, the really passionate ones will even do your advertising for you — by being vocal advocates of your product or service to friends, relatives, colleagues and acquaintances.

The test of the strength of a customer's loyalty tends to be if he or she will stick with your brand over and above a competitor's, even when there is a rational reason (price, convenience, color) to switch. As they say in the retail trade, loyalty is "the extent to which your customer will continue to buy more from you, even when your competitors are offering more attractive prices, products or services".

Emotional vs behavioral loyalty

If we are to fully understand this concept of loyalty from a marketing point of view, it is important at this stage that we distinguish between two very different types of loyalty — *behavioral* loyalty and *emotional* loyalty.

- **Behavioral Loyalty**

  This is simply observed behavior, from data or research. It looks for observed patterns of behavior — such as retention rates at a bank, or frequency of visits at a retail outlet, or the dollar-value of online purchases at an e-store.

  However reassuring such quantitative substantiation might be, it doesn't even begin to assess the question "why" certain people are behaving in this manner.

  To demonstrate this, KPMG, a consulting firm, has devised a "Loyalty Ladder" which shows clearly how simple "observed loyalty" could in fact be the result of a whole host of different motivations. It shows how unreliable topline loyalty data could be. The KPMG ladder categorizes customers as follows:

a) *The Vampire*

This customer is on the bottom of the loyalty ladder. What looks from the data to be a friendly, money-spending customer is really something much worse — they are only looking for special deals. They appear to be loyal, but have no real affinity for the brand at all.

b) *The Indifferent*

This is the customer who looks loyal on paper — "behaviorally" — (a frequent visitor, for example), but has no feelings about your brand whatsoever. How can you spot one of these from your till-receipts?

c) *The Hostage*

As the name suggests, these customers, for whatever reason, are trapped into buying your brand. Perhaps they are accruing "loyalty points"; perhaps they have to buy your brand because it's the only one available. Whatever the reason, they are starting to feel highly negative about having to buy your brand, which is bad news for your business.

d) *The Terrorist*

Hostages become terrorists who bad-mouth your brand at every turn. This is the road to nowhere.

e) *The Bad-Habit Buyer*

These customers may purchase frequently but, each time they do, they build increasingly bad will towards you and your brand. This could be due to product quality, lack of choice or even poor service. They are locked into a bad habit. Surely, they are going to kick it one day soon?

f) *The "Waiting for a Better Deal" Buyer*

These customers are exhibiting what would clearly show up on any research data as behavioral loyalty. *But*, they are just staying with the brand while waiting for something else to come along! When it does, they will then gladly and quickly shift over. Numbers don't reveal motivation.

g) *The Mercenary*

This happens a lot — a company buys a customer's loyalty with points or rewards. Customers may feel locked into an offering which does not totally satisfy them, and they feel little *genuine* affinity with the brand or service. They can give the brand owner a sense of false security ("Look at how many 'loyal' customers we have!"). Furthermore, lengthy payback periods (involving, for example, 10 purchases of an infrequently bought product) can create ill-will with the customer, who feels a strong obligation to use your brand even if they don't want to.

h) *The Admirer and Special-Occasion Buyer*

These are customers who have seldom (if ever) made a purchase of your brand, but have a strong affinity for it. They could be valuable in the future, or they could be instrumental in retaining your brand currency amongst a consumer franchise that *is* buying your brand.

i) *The True Loyalist*

This is the ideal loyalty state, creating an unbreakable connection with the customer. This might typically be achieved through a combination of behavioral consistency and strong emotional affiliation. These customers are buying your brand repeatedly because they are "emotionally loyal" to it. Let us explain a little more about emotional loyalty.

- **Emotional Loyalty**

  There is traditionally little room in business for "feelings". We prefer data, reports, analysis, facts. Yet, at the same time, we are hearing more and more about the need to "take the brand into the boardroom".

  Chairmen and CEOs are increasingly becoming aware that their vast empires of factories, outlets, staff, financing deals, supply chains, value chains, distribution and logistics networks only exist because of the *brand*. Without the brand, customer appeal dries up, sales dry up, factories close, boardrooms get cleaned out. An oft-quoted fact: in 1950, 99% of the value of all companies listed on the New York Stock Exchange was measured in tangible assets. In 2000, 60% of the value of the NYSE was measured in *intangible* assets — these days, the brand has a huge value in the boardroom.

And yet, brands are nothing but a collection of *feelings* that a customer has about a product or a service. Yes, to a greater or lesser extent, those feelings can be influenced by marketing. But at the heart of a brand is a one-on-one *relationship* between an individual and that brand, and a relationship is something that can be quite personal.

As with any other type of relationship, the depth of the relationship between the individual and the brand, the level of affinity each has for the other, differs from person to person. Emotional loyalty is simply the measure of how close (or distant) an individual feels towards a brand. And it is this measurement of "feeling" that ought to be one of the most important corporate measures available.

In the last chapter, we talked about how a 360 Degree Branding® campaign will only be successful long term if it is based on a powerful, enduring Idea.

Ideas involve people by making connections between product benefits, consumer needs and the way they see their world. An Idea creates what we call *emotional bonding*. It makes people feel the brand promise, and believe in the brand. It has the power to make things seem simple when they are not, or add a depth of meaning to things we often take for granted.

This requires a deep, relentless probing for insights (which we deal with in the next chapter). We need to understand what is a brand's attraction to its users; what drives its reputation; what actually matters to them in the broad series of associations, feelings and memories; how the brand is unique in the relationships it builds.

Once we have identified the emotional reward a brand brings people, we can work it into a series of executional ideas that form and reinforce that sense of emotional bonding.

It is that simple. It is that precious. (And it is that hard).

The pyramid of affinity

To help us unravel this concept of emotional loyalty, there is a simple model we can use. The BrandZ model, developed by WPP's Millward Brown, and now the world's largest database of its kind, incorporates data collected since 1998. A total of 260,000 consumers have been surveyed in 27 countries, covering relationships with 70 product categories and 10,000 global and key local brands. It is an ongoing study, which is repeated every year to build up a picture over time.

It is therefore the most comprehensive study ever undertaken into understanding how and why consumers buy brands. The study provides an invaluable database about consumers' buying behavior, and a simple measure of the depth of their loyalty to one brand or another. This is shown as a pyramid.

The levels of the pyramid categorize the level of emotional loyalty each customer has with a brand.

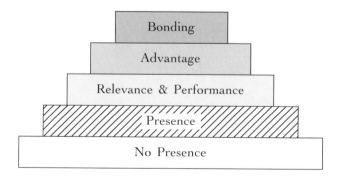

Level 1 — No Presence

Some consumers may know little or nothing about a brand. A category buyer at "No Presence" has absolutely no emotional loyalty for the brand. They have never tried the brand, are not spontaneously aware of it, and are not familiar with its promise.

Level 2 — Presence

"Presence", the second level, is the starting point for emotional loyalty. The brand is familiar to the consumer. Consumers have tried the brand, or are spontaneously aware of it, or know about its promise. They are likely to have some emotional loyalty to the brand, but it is still at a low level.

Level 3 — Relevance and Performance

At the third level, emotional loyalty strengthens. The consumer has positive feelings about the brand and no overriding negative feelings. Category buyers at "Relevance and Performance" have a moderate degree of emotional loyalty for the brand. They believe the brand can meet their needs, is at about the right price, is their kind of brand, and performs its job adequately.

Level 4 — Advantage

"Advantage" is the fourth level. The brand is one of the consumer's favorites. A category buyer at this level has a high degree of emotional loyalty for the brand, rating the brand highly on at least one differentiating attribute.

Level 5 — Bonding

"Bonding" is the fifth and final level, where true emotional loyalty is achieved. The brand is the consumer's "preferred brand". A category buyer at this level has the ultimate degree of emotional loyalty — in some ways they feel they "own" the brand. Consumers at "Bonding" rate the brand highly on many attributes and they often recommend it to others.

All things being equal (that is, it is available, it fits their particular needs at the point of purchase, no competing brand is making an absurdly low price offer, etc), consumers at this level will buy your brand.

Bonding is the peak of the pyramid. A customer who bonds with a brand is the one that exhibits the greatest emotional loyalty to a brand. They *feel* a strong affinity for this brand. They believe it not only delivers what it says it will, it stands for something a consumer is prepared to believe in. It has values and a personality that the consumer finds attractive — almost to the exclusion of competing brands.

The financial value of emotional loyalty

It is also possible to quantify the *value* that a bonded customer adds to a brand. This value *directly* influences things like brand leadership, market share, customer-retention rates and even repeat-purchase behavior. In this way, we can easily connect strong brands with actual dollars and cents. There is a direct link between the *depth of emotional loyalty* and the amount that the customer *spends on that brand*.

While working with the BrandZ data, Ogilvy has developed a proprietary tool for understanding the financial value of emotional loyalty. As part of this, the company has uncovered six universal truths.

Six universal truths about emotional loyalty

Truth #1: The greater the Emotional Loyalty, the greater the customer's financial value.

A buyer's financial value to a brand grows substantially as their emotional loyalty for a brand increases. For example, a customer who is positioned at Advantage level on the pyramid (the second-highest level) is generally worth *double* the value of a customer who is still at the bottom (Presence level).

90

Truth #2: *Value leaps dramatically when Bonding is achieved.*
Move one further rung up the pyramid — from Advantage to Bonding — and customer's financial value to a brand grows exponentially as their emotional loyalty peaks at Bonding. Customers increase in value *another three or four times* between Advantage and Bonding. A brand buyer at Bonding is generally worth almost *10 times* as much as the average buyer at Presence.

Ten times … think about it.

Truth #3: *All Bonded consumers are not created equal.*
All consumers on the survey, regardless of their emotional attachment to a brand, can be classified into three purchase categories — heavy, medium and light. What is interesting to note is that not all heavy buyers are bonded. Likewise, not all bonded consumers are heavy users — it's perfectly easy to conceive of a light user who is nonetheless emotionally bonded to a brand.

When it comes to looking for the most valuable consumers, we simply look to correlate "heavy users" with "bonded users". Unsurprisingly, the most valuable consumers, by a substantial margin, are heavy users — the high-value segment — who *also bond* with the brand. High-value customers who are also emotionally bonded to a brand can be worth *12 to 15 times* as much as the average buyer at Presence.

The stakes keep getting higher.

Truth #4: *Bonding is extremely difficult to achieve.*
Only about 5% of all brands worldwide manage to bond with 20% of their customers. The average Bonding level for all brands is only about 5% of their buyers. Consumers generally reach the Advantage level of the pyramid for two to three brands, but virtually never bond with more than one. Many consumers do not bond at all.

Truth #5: Bonding is a key driver of brand leadership.

It has long been proven (via expensive panel studies) that the brand with the most "heavy users" (what we call the high-value users) is usually the brand leader. This behavioral insight can now be enhanced by adding to it this study of emotional loyalty.

The brand that manages to create the highest levels of emotional bonding is virtually always the brand leader. The margin of brand leadership is often the additional sales contributed by bonded brand buyers, especially high-value bonded consumers. So if you want to be number one in a market or category, this would suggest that you need to invest in building a 360 Degree brand that will create high levels of emotional loyalty.

Truth #6: Bonding keeps loyal buyers loyal.

Finally, emotional loyalty significantly reduces attrition. Or, to put it another way, emotional loyalty significantly increases retention.

High-value customers own more of the brand

It is important not to lose sight of the fact that although bonded customers are far more valuable than all others, they are also exceedingly rare. (BrandZ data shows that only 5% of the average brand's customers are bonded). It is also difficult — without interviewing every single purchaser — to know who they are, and therefore how to invest against their value. Fortunately, however, there is an obvious correlation between high-value customers, and customers who are bonded to the brand. The Italian philosopher Pareto made the observation that 20% of the customers account for 80% of the sales. Over the past 10 years we have been testing this in action around the world, and what is extraordinary is just how universal this rule is — in everything from denim to coffee to air travel to financial services.

This accounts for the huge investments which are now made in programs to acquire, bond and retain high-value customers. By developing direct channels of communication and a sense of recognition and privilege, the brand message can be intensified, and the bond can be guarded with the few customers who will make or break the brand. For this reason it is clearly misguided to see your advertising as "brand building" and your direct marketing as a sales-closer. With a 360 Degree mindset, both are brand-building activities.

It is important to remember that high-value customers often have a rather different perception and experience of the brand, and therefore traditional communications can actually repel, rather than attract, them. A simple message, meant for a mass audience, can seem patronising and demeaning to a loyal customer. (In one case, for a high street chemist in the UK, we discovered that the loyal customers used the shop in an entirely different way. Rather than dashing in, making a few, pre-determined purchases and then leaving in five minutes, they would spend half an hour digging in the back of the shop to see what else was on offer. They understood far more about the way the company wanted the shop to be, rather than the way it was really seen by the mass market. Therefore, communications designed especially for them, as an engaged audience, paid disproportionate dividends.)

Loyalty and 360 Degree brand communications

We can clearly see just how vital (and financially rewarding) it is to create emotional loyalty and sustain high levels of Bonded consumers at the top of your brand pyramid. The term "Bonding" may be new, but even David Ogilvy could see its power: "Successful brands are those which build bonds with the consumer."

So, how do we go about establishing those bonds? It may help to understand the nature of bonds that the customer may have with the brand, and their relative strengths and weaknesses. One way to categorize them is to look at those bonds which are *structural*, vis-a-vis those which are *emotional*.

Structural bonds are disincentives for the customer to change. They may be financial and negative (i.e. a financial cost of switching which makes the customer reluctant to change) or they may be physical and positive (i.e. an embedded home delivery service). Either way, they give the customer a rational reason to stay loyal. Emotional bonds are far harder to create, but also far more sustainable against competition. When someone talks about "my brand" they are generally displaying a level of emotional bonding. Emotional bonds are the demonstrators of true loyalty. Structural bonds are effective, but appeal to the pragmatic or mercenary side of human nature. Of course, these bonds are not mutually exclusive, as is shown by this chart of potential relationships:

Behavioral loyalty		Emotional loyalty	
High	prisoners	good friends	happy marriages
Medium	neighbors	colleagues	courtship
Low	enquirers	extended families	distant lovers
	Low	**Medium**	**High**

Are 360 Degree brand communications better at creating and sustaining emotional brand loyalty than mono-media solutions? The answer is a resounding "Yes", and for very good reasons.

From the previous section, it should be clear that a key objective of almost any brand's communications is to turn "occasional users" into "loyalists", and eventually into "advocates" — building "bonding", the top of the pyramid, in other words.

Interestingly, there is no *one* simple factor that is responsible for creating affinity or bonding. Every time consumers encounter the brand, it makes an impact on their subconscious — from quality, to taste, to packaging, to line extensions, to the retail environment, to the showroom, to the lobby, to ergonomics, design and color, to sales promotions, price and product displays, to sponsorships and joint ventures, to corporate reputations, public relations and environmental policy, to the sales force and service experiences, to the labels, to the brands it shares shelf space with, to the delivery trucks, to the website, to word-of-mouth, to telemarketing scripts and receptionists' style, to the way the telephone is answered and complaints are handled, to overarching prejudices and societal attitudes, to collective and individual memories, to history.

If you are not managing a majority of these, then you are not really managing anything.

It is the consumer's experience of the brand, in all its manifestations and at every point of contact, that creates the brand relationship, that determines whether it is positive or negative, that builds emotional loyalty and market share.

Great brands inspire great loyalty

Great brands (which means profitable brands, with high numbers of emotionally loyal consumers) are almost always 360 Degree brands. That is because makers of great brands know they don't own the brand; the consumer does. But they also know that they, as the manufacturer, are responsible for how that brand lives and breathes in the consumer's life. The brand must be reflected in everything that touches the consumer. To give the consumer a 360 Degree experience means the brand must live and breathe beyond its narrowly defined "loyalty programs". A wonderful example of this comes from one of Asia's best known brands — *Brand's*.

CASE STUDY 4

Cerebos and *Brand's* — Creating a customer-centric business

This case study gives a fascinating insight into how one leading Asian multinational has re-engineered its business and marketing to focus on building customer loyalty. In this respect (and in many others too), Cerebos is at the cutting-edge of a new type of Asian brand, one which is moving away from a reliance on traditional mass-marketing techniques, to focus on highly sophisticated, technology-enabled, "one-to-one" communications with existing and potential customers, to secure their loyalty and their advocacy.

Unlike some of the other case studies in this book, this is not a "brand story" with a beginning, a middle and an end. Rather, this is very much an evolving and ongoing corporate narrative. While it may have had a catalyst in a new brand positioning, the corporate-wide change of emphasis to a "customer-centric" business is not a short-term or finite experiment, but an initiative that has permeated every facet of the organization. Furthermore, it shows why Cerebos (and *Brand's*) can serve as a beacon to other Asian companies by demonstrating such a forward-thinking and sophisticated approach to marketing.

History

Cerebos Pacific Limited can trace its name back to 1892 when a French chemical engineer decided to mix calcium phosphate with salt, and promptly invented dry-pouring salt. The brand name "Cerebos" was subsequently registered, the name being derived from "Ceres" (the Roman goddess of the wheat harvest), and "os" (from the French word for "bone" that the phosphates in salt strengthen). Cerebos subsequently grew to include a wide range of food products. It acquired Brand & Company in 1959.

"*Brand's*" is the now-famous health supplement brand with which many consumers in Asia, particularly Chinese consumers, will be extremely familiar. The first *Brand's* health supplement was invented way back in 1835, by a chef to the British Royal Family. Mr. H.W. Brand worked in Buckingham Palace during the reign of King George IV. Concerned about the King's ailing health, Mr. Brand decided to improve on the age-old chicken soup remedy by creating a fat-free, easily digested chicken consommé. That was the very first batch of "*Brand's* Essence of Chicken".

In 1920, the first shipment arrived in Asia, and *Brand's* has been part of the landscape ever since. Part of the reason why *Brand's* caught on so fast was its similarity to a local Asian "double-boiled" chicken essence, widely used for centuries as a health tonic. Not only was *Brand's* a convenient, 100% natural, packaged version of the traditional remedy, it was also seen as healthier due to the fact that it was completely fat-free, unlike grandmother's chicken soup.

Brand's Essence of Chicken is Cerebos' flagship product, and is the category leader in Thailand, Taiwan, Singapore, Malaysia, Hong Kong and China. More than 100 million bottles of *Brand's* products were sold last year.

Traditional approach

Like many packaged-goods companies in Asia (and indeed worldwide), *Brand's* had developed a fairly traditional approach to marketing. Essentially, this was based on mass communications, mainly press and television advertising. It also had a newsletter that went to its known customers whose names had been collected through local events. And, for many years, this approach was successful and represented a commitment to an integrated approach to the brand.

However, the marketplace is a constantly evolving playing field, and consumers are known to be changeable creatures. The healthcare supplement category in Asia was becoming more sophisticated, and more saturated. New players, from traditional Chinese medicines that were being successfully packaged and branded, to technologically advanced formats imported from Australia and New Zealand, were crowding the marketplace and changing consumers' expectations.

Brand's Essence of Chicken was a traditional liquid supplement that was being used by consumers as an occasional "pick-me-up". While the brand's most loyal customers used it as a regular health supplement for preventative purposes, the occasional users were (potentially) under threat from new formats and brands. Cerebos correctly identified the need to reposition *Brand's* for these consumers as something more than just an occasional treatment.

A new positioning

In conjunction with a whole new range of products and formats, from vitamin supplements to natural extracts, *Brand's* was re-launched under the positioning "Health Partner for Life". As part of this new positioning process, Cerebos encouraged the greater use of many and newer marketing disciplines to support its investment: Public Relations, online and interactive Web marketing, and a much wider role and definition for one-to-one direct communications. In evaluating which would be the right marketing techniques to sustain its brand business model, Cerebos came up against three important issues.

Three key issues

Firstly, one of the most important areas for growth was from existing users, through encouraging them to increase their frequency of purchase, or to increase their breadth of purchase. For these customers, *Brand's* needed to be a true "health partner". By default, therefore, communicating more intimately with these people through one-to-one brand communications was becoming increasingly important.

Secondly, as the market matured and consumers were being exposed to more and more health messages, those health messages were becoming less and less effective. Plenty of research studies showed that consumers did not necessarily trust the voice of the manufacturer to give them unbiased health advice, preferring word-of-mouth and the endorsement of medical professionals, parents and reliable (trusted) magazines. CRM techniques were therefore seen as crucial in establishing, firstly, the trust of the customer, then their loyalty and, finally, their advocacy — allowing them to spread the word-of-mouth to others.

Finally, Cerebos found it increasingly difficult to quantify the effectiveness of mass-marketing techniques. As its marketing model moved more towards harnessing the purchasing power of its existing customers, so the need for mass communications waned.

The new Customer Relationship Management Team was therefore set up to provide quality and professional customer service for retaining valued customers and enhancing total customer satisfaction, and has become the driving force behind *Brand's* as a "health partner".

The new approach

For the first time, *Brand's* began to actively segment (and then communicate with) customers based on their usage habits and needs. It sought to build extensive profiles of its customers, and to gain active and actionable feedback from them on all sorts of topics; from formulation, to distribution, to packaging.

Three core infrastructures were developed — a call centre in each market, a website (www.brandsworld.com), and an ongoing one-to-one direct marketing communications program.

The website was designed to offer that all-important ingredient in the healthcare category — information, as well as expert opinions, news and updates. The web functions as a hub for many of the brand's activities, and was established to embody the idea of "health partnership". It provides ample opportunity for a two-way conversation with the brand. The call centres, backed up by sophisticated data-management technology, serve as the frontline in customer service. While the one-to-one marketing collateral is mainly targeted at key user-groups, and is designed to keep those users feeling involved and important to the brand.

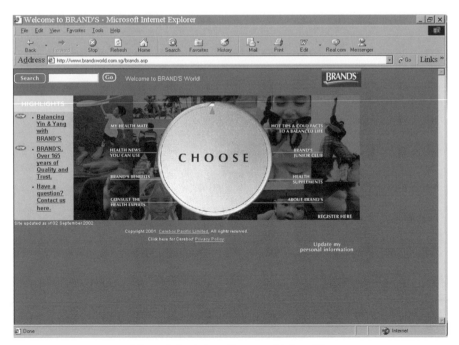

The website brings "partnership" to life

Beyond the marketing department

The company began to realize that such a commitment to CRM could neither be short-term nor confined to the marketing department. It needed to become part of the fabric of the entire organization. Senior management embraced the CRM initiative, and it spread to all areas of the firm — from finance, to sales, to research and development, to distribution and even the technical support staff. Customer-focused training has been implemented across a wide spectrum of the firm's activities, and continues to be so. As Cerebos has shown, CRM and loyalty programs are long-term beliefs that manifest themselves as ways of thinking, not just programs of activities.

Implications

The adoption of a loyalty focused strategy has three key implications for any business embracing 360 Degree marketing. First, the entire business has become an evolving, learning and iterative process. By listening to customers, by being able to try new selling techniques with customers, by looking at patterns of purchase and interest, the business has become orientated around perpetual improvement. And, as a result, the brand has gone on to create even

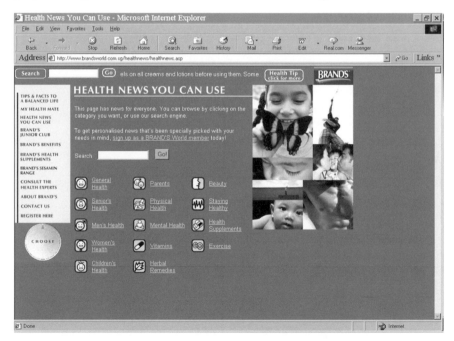

The Brand's *website has become a focal point for a customer-centric strategy*
(Reproduced with kind permission of Cerebos)

stronger loyalty by being able to show that it really is listening and learning from its customers.

Second, *Brand's* has had to re-examine its attitudes to mass marketing communications. Whereas before, these had been default activities, now *Brand's* is having to re-look at the role they play in its business, whether that be increasing the overall user-base, or maintaining levels of brand equity. Either way, it has made the role of mass communications more accountable, by questioning its role in the marketing mix, and has made the company think about the brand, not just in a traditional way, but as a part of a customer-centric business model.

And third, Cerebos has shown through its example how a loyalty-based initiative needs to be a corporate-wide practice. As such, it is a shining example of how important it is for "brand" to be a business issue, not simply a marketing issue. The brand needs to permeate all aspects of the operation, in order to maximize its potential.

Conclusion

For Cerebos, this has meant devoting increasing energy to Customer Relationship Management. However, the company provides a wonderful example of how CRM does not mean just a website; or just a direct mail shot; or just a telesales call. Rather (and this is at the very heart of their brand thinking), *everything is CRM* — everything a company does, from packaging to product development, to distribution to customer care, should all be about managing customer relationships. Having realized this, Cerebos is a long way down the journey to being one of the very few truly Asian customer-centric organizations, with a brand that commands great loyalty and great respect.

FOLK EVENTS IN SRI LANKA

Sri Lanka has a rich tradition of indigenous communication forms which somewhat pre-date the conventional media channels of the West. Some of these communication forms have been revived and used by brands, especially in rural markets, which make up 70% of Sri Lanka's population.

Perahera (cultural pageant)
The *perahera* is a pageant linked to many religious and cultural ceremonies. It is made up of various colorful dance forms and traditional music. The resounding, pulsating rhythms of the different drums make it quite an experience.

The *perahera* form has recently been reinvented for the modern communication age — an age-old tradition being used for brand communications. What it achieves is a memorable and unique way to interact with people. The pageant moves through the streets to a strategic location. Competitions and entertainment are organized as part of the event.

Street drama
Another traditional medium being used for modern brand purposes is street drama, where a popular dramatist acts out a story. More stand-up comedy than "advertising", this form of media is a great attraction for rural audiences who have very limited entertainment options.

Viridu (ballad)
This is another form of popular entertainment in regional towns. A balladeer recites poetry to the rhythm of a hand-held drum. Marketers have used this as a media entertainment tool to sell their products in these regions. They perform in crowd-gathering locations such as bus and train terminals, and in market squares in the main towns.

Shanthi Karma (rain dance)
This is a typical Sri Lankan ritual practiced mainly by farming communities to seek the blessings of the rain gods and to ask for early and timely rain. The best example of how brands have used this to their advantage in recent years was organized by Singer, a brand that sells farming equipment. At that time, Sri Lanka was suffering from severe droughts. In perhaps the finest example of "corporate social responsibility", Singer's rain dance brought torrential showers the very next day.

Shanthi Karma *in Sri Lanka*

7

Discovery is a Due Diligence

"Discovery is seeing what everybody has seen, and thinking what nobody has thought."
Albert Nagyrapolt, Nobel Prize-winning physicist

Data and repetition

Most people are seduced by the exercise of data-gathering almost as an end in itself. But *volume* of data and *value* of data are almost invariably at opposite ends of the spectrum.

Volume of data encourages repetition. The data only tells us "this is how things were"; it also indicates how, all things being equal, things will continue to be. People tend to look for reassurance in data and therefore expect consistency in findings. This creates an incredible amount of inertia.

The law of inertia imposes a dull consistency on the world of business. If we keep on doing the same old things, we may sustain brand awareness, maintain a truly loyal base of customers, support third-party endorsement, keep sales ticking over. But, this will not create the conditions for a more powerful brand position to evolve over time.

The value of data lies in the inconsistencies we see between findings: the differences between people, the way they use a product, react to a stimulus, receive a message. People do extraordinary things, if you watch them closely. Data never lies, but it rarely tells you things straight. There are always hidden meanings. And numbers can tell us the best stories of all, if we reverse the normal way of looking at them.

Discovery is never ending

A well-known universal law is that everything tends to chaos — this is called entropy. It is an important principle. Much of the time, so-called brand stewards seem to operate under the delusion that they are actually controlling a brand. The entire premise of 360 Degree brand building suggests otherwise. The brand–consumer relationship is constantly evolving, constantly being adapted by the myriad influences and interactions a consumer has with the brand and its competitors.

Because of this constantly diverging, entropic world we live in, Discovery *must* be an ongoing exercise, a never-ending pursuit, a way of life, a mindset. It is not something that merely occurs at the beginning of the development process. Taking short cuts is bad for the brand and bad for business.

"Some Agencies scorn research and homework. They skid about on the slippery surface of irrelevant brilliance. We, on the other hand, prefer the discipline of knowledge to the anarchy of ignorance. We pursue knowledge the way a pig pursues truffles."

David Ogilvy

The path of Discovery (and re-discovery) is not simply a linear process that can be slotted in between briefs (after the client one, and before the creative one). Contrary to popular opinion, positioning is not something that is carved in stone — it is something that exists in the consumer's mind, always adapting and being adapted to fit the changing world.

New ideas in technology, economics, marketing, retail, culture and just about any field have direct repercussions across the entire world of ideas. Everything is affected by everything else — style, fashion, fads, rumor, gossip, and the occasional urban myth are all major influences on brands.

That brand–consumer relationship you thought you understood? All change, please! Once you accept the plurality of a 360 Degree brand world, you commit yourself to an endless process of Discovery. And nothing could be more invigorating.

The tools of Discovery

The famous spy novelist John le Carré once said: "A desk is a dangerous place from which to observe the world." It takes intelligence to gather intelligence. We need to uncover the "private eye" within us, and get out and rub shoulders with our "target audience" (also known as "people", by the way!).

This task can be approached in a number of ways:

- **Data grazing**

  Data is the lifeblood of our business. We need to know how to capture data, how to access it, how to make sense of it and how to use it well.

  This is not as easy as it sounds. Data is also the sludge of the Information Age. As the world becomes ever-more complicated, we are all exposed to (and buried under) more and more data. The raw data we use is almost always available to our competitors.

  The trick is to be patient. Gather all the facts. Be thorough. Don't assume that because the clients say they have no data that there is no data available. They probably say this because the data they have is not properly classified, or they don't understand why we want it.

  Even if the client hands us mountains of the stuff, the point is that there is much more, and quite possibly more useful, stuff that we can gather from other sources as well. We should immerse ourselves in anything and everything that can possibly have a bearing on the brand.

Visits with the sales force, analyzing sales data, usage and attitude studies, tracking studies and qualitative research are all valuable. But they won't tell us everything we need to know. Tangible, first-hand observation is as important as the most expensive research analysis.

- **Observation**

  Old-style research techniques are all very well. But why depend on paid researchers to come over to the office to tell us what's going on outside? We have eyes and ears — and five other senses! Furthermore, research is a very blunt tool, developed to explain and rationalize; it is not equipped to handle the irrational or the illogical.

  There are endless opportunities to get inside the minds and lives of consumers — to illuminate the "invisible downtime" of people, and identify the opportunities for a brand to make connections with them. They all involve leaving the safety of the office to actually watch what is happening where it is happening.

  It is not difficult, and should not be beyond anyone, to do some real, human Discovery. Survive for a day on the same budget your consumer does; compare the differences between women's shopping lists with their receipts; hitch a

---

UNDERSTANDING THE CORE CONSUMER

A sunglasses manufacturer wanted to know why his brand of glasses was seen as un-cool by cool, urban, male teenagers, an important consumer target. After close observation, the Discovery team noted that it had nothing to do with the brand's design, color, shade or brand reputation. In store, lanky teenagers were forced to stoop low to check that they looked cool, because the shades were perched (as they always wore them) on the top of their heads.

A simple recommendation to angle the mirrors at 45 degrees, rather than hang them vertically, had a major impact on sales.

lift with truckers for three days to get a "feel" for their lives (as a Japanese CEO of a canned-coffee brand did recently); or just take a different route to work every day for a week, and check out what is going on.

- **Hypothesis**

  Having gathered data and observations, you need to be able to map them out and start to create some initial hypotheses. Which bits of information have given you a better understanding of a brand or its category? In what way does this new information modify your perceptions? What implications does this knowledge have for decisions and actions? What might you have to do to convince others of its importance?

  Data and observation in isolation, however, can be dangerous stuff. Dislocated from culture and behavioral patterns, it can take on unwarranted meaning. There are other tools too for putting data and observation into a wider cultural context. These might include laddering (keep asking: "What is the benefit of the benefit?"); cultural anthropology (to identify the big social trends); linguistics (how the shape and style of language is used by different types of consumer); popular culture (what the major influences of the day are); counter culture (what the innovators and early adopters are doing); and semiotics (how various signs and symbols are being interpreted by the people who see them).

  All these, and many others, help us to avoid over-rational interpretation of research, and to hypothesize the deeper meanings that give us the inspiration to have Ideas.

- **Context**

  Think of a brand. What category is it operating in? Sounds simple? Not always so.

  The client's definition of their business is usually a simple category definition: carbonated soft-drinks; ice teas; airlines;

etc. This does not help you, because a category definition only describes the nature of the product. You need to know what need the product fulfills; for example, you are in the thirst-quenching business for a soft-drinks manufacturer, or the business of carrying people to meet each other for an airline.

But even then, defining the "consumer need" the product fulfills only gives us the generic platform for brand communications. If nothing else, it will make our communication relevant. But it won't give us a competitive advantage, and that is what all brand communications need to do.

Thinking differently about the category can also help us think differently about what our brand offers its customers (its benefits, users, packaging elements, use of colors, price, distribution, the way people use the product or service, its communications strategy or investment, market share and so on).

You can retain the current category definition. Or you can narrow it. Or you can broaden it. By making this simple choice you can get real insight into how to position the brand.

Here is an example of narrowing a category. Ask yourself: What are diamonds?

We could classify diamonds in the category of gems, jewelry, or big gifts, or investments, or major purchases — depending on whether you were assessing them according to looks, function, type of purchase or value. But, in each case, we would be missing out on the very distinctive emotional reward: giving a diamond as a gift reinforces an important bond between two people who love each other very much. No other product can replicate this. It is unique and therefore exists in a category of one.

Now, consider the following example of broadening a category.

Ask yourself, what is Coca-Cola? Does it belong to the category of foreign colas, or carbonated soft-drinks, or all soft drinks, or all packaged beverages? The options seem endless. And exploring them all can be a worthwhile exercise. In some markets, Coca-Cola is classified as a "snack product". The logic goes like this: Coke is mostly drunk when people want a little something to fill their stomach, not when they are thirsty. People therefore consider a Coke as something to be chosen instead of a chocolate bar or an ice-cream or a packet of crisps.

By deciding to narrow or broaden the category definition, we may understand something deeper about the product that we might otherwise miss. In the process, we might uncover a whole host of positioning (or Strategic Idea) alternatives and hence stimulus for differentiated brand ideas.

- **Changing the focus of observation**
  Change is the norm, not the exception. Thus, it is important to explore the wider marketplace issues and market conditions. A brand needs to relate to factors outside its immediate control.

  In Asia, focus groups are notoriously difficult to extract meaningful insight from (the respondents are too aware of the marketing spotlight being thrown on them to act naturally) and they rely entirely on "claimed behavior", which is no good for uncovering "unguarded moments".

> *"I love doing those discussion group things — you get to tell them which ads to make."*
>
> *Indra, 19, Singapore*

As we all know, nice girls don't talk to strangers! Vast swathes of people's ordinary lives remain hidden from marketers. To uncover these "secret lives", an alternative way of looking at the world is required.

Pablo Picasso's deliberate distortions of human and animal faces were not born purely out of his imagination, but from a deep and close-up examination of the faces of his various mistresses. From a distance of a couple of centimeters, apparently, if one looks very closely, this is the perspective one gets.

Playing the role of observer in business is important, both for seeing what is out there in the world affecting our brand, and for adding that impartial, objective point of view that only "outsiders" can give an account team.

The P–C–E relationship

There are only three things we need to observe well for us to create better ideas: the Product, the Consumer, and the Environment in which they exist. Most importantly, we need to observe the *interaction* between them, because it is the dynamic interaction between the Product, the Consumer and the Environment that sparks the Challenge and, hence, the Idea.

Consumer–Product interaction

Here we look for triggers that reflect the *"unchanging values"* (as articulated in the BrandPrint). As we know, this is where "product" becomes "brand". But simply capturing and reflecting (or even building on) the unchanging values will not be stimulating enough, without including the *changing* associations and expectations of the brand experience.

For example, Nike has been built up over the past two decades as probably the most celebrated example of brand building. We all feel that we should "Just do it", and the brand's whole resonance and inner meaning is captured in a simple swoosh.

However, relationships change. Now, even "your mother wears Nike" (as one of Nike's competitors forcefully reminded us just a few years ago). And the newspapers recently have been full of stories to do with unethical work practices. Nike is an example of a brand that continued to promote its brand core when it should perhaps have been looking at the Product–Consumer and Product–Environment interactions and made some significant changes.

The reason why we need to examine this interaction is the fact that the consumer can be very fickle. Adidas has had a tremendous revival over the past four or five years and has captured the icon appeal of the up-and-coming generation.

Let's consider another major brand: IBM. While the "Solutions for a Small Planet" campaign helped restore IBM's fundamental image in the marketplace, the emergence of the Internet threatened to leave IBM in the dust. IBM could not compete with the young, hip Internet start-ups who were using a generic "We're on the Net" message.

But consider this: the Internet was about networked computers. IBM knew networked computers better than anyone. The Internet was about massive transaction volumes, security and scalability. Again, IBM was the leader. And, most importantly, IBM's customers, business and IT leaders wanted to use the Internet for business, not browsing. With this observation, IBM could own the part of the Internet where real business took place.

The IBM inspiration was to give it a name and an identity — "e-business" — and then build a business and a communications strategy around it: e-business consulting teams; e-business products and services; e-business business models; and integrated, pervasive e-business communications.

Environment—Consumer interaction

Here, we are really examining the impact of the marketplace on the brand. By "marketplace" we mean:

- the context in which people are exposed to brand messages — when and in what circumstances they come into contact with our brand messages
- what is on their minds — the trends, fads, fashions, the things that grab a disproportionate mind-share of our target's lives
- how the outlets (or places) where our target meets the physical brand look and feel, and how our brand is displayed in them
- the social conditions that people live in (think of China and all the "one child" families — do they all look alike and live in similar ways, and have similar agendas?).

Social policy can have a big potential impact on a brand's development. So too can the media in its broadest sense — what people consume, how, when, where and why. We need to get a feel for the qualitative aspects of the type of information and entertainment they are exposed to, and how they are feeling when they consume it.

For example, in Thailand, during the 1997–98 recession there was a major shift in Thailand's beer market from mainstream to low-priced beers. This was good news for Leo, a low-priced beer bought in bulk.

Here, the marketing objective was simple: get people to order more Leo beer for their parties. However, the opportunity was wider than that. In a depressing economic climate, the customer needs an outlet for fun, as well as value for money. The team intuitively knew this, and turned the objective around, defining the Challenge as: "Leo beer turns every drinking occasion into party-time."

Thus, the brand idea was to transform numerous classic drinking occasions — weddings, New Year celebrations, reunions, job offers, the birth of a son — into "party-time". The team then exploited everything from concert tours and sports events to beer festivals.

Product–Environment interaction

Here, we reverse the question: "How could the brand change the nature of the marketplace? And how does it provoke curiosity?"

Can single brands change marketplaces? Sure they can, and do; frequently. Take, for example, the phenomenon of increased mobility through the 20th century.

At the beginning of the century, Henry Ford spotted the phenomenon and provoked his potential customer to think differently about horsepower. "If I had asked my customers what they really wanted," he said, "they would have said a faster horse."

A couple of decades later, cars were established conveyances — to do the shopping, to make deliveries and to undertake other important local business activities. However, if you were a tire manufacturer, it took ages before people came to visit you for a new tire. The trick here was to help people see that their cars were something more than merely functional — they could also be a means to explore more of their world. Hence the Michelin Motoring Guides, that encouraged folk to get out and see (and taste!) more. More driving meant having to replace tires more often. Voilá! Sell the pleasure, profit from the pain!

In the late 1970s, Sony's Akio Morita realized that people often traveled alone for long periods, with little source of personal entertainment. And so the Sony Walkman was born.

A decade later came a means of keeping in touch wherever you are — the mobile phone.

With the rise of the Internet, in response to people's increased mobility, a whole host of new opportunities to do things on the move was spawned. The Challenge for E*Trade, for example, was to eradicate every traditional barrier that comes between individuals and their ability to trade freely.

And, in the new millennium, we have witnessed the amazing phenomenon of i-mode in Japan, and Short Messaging Services in a number of Asian markets.

This, in turn, has opened up a whole host of new brand communications opportunities to match the changing environment. Now, we can push customers to the point of sale during off-peak periods for McDonald's in Australia or locate potential Nescafé customers in Japan during their coffee break. The key to success lies in understanding how people use communication in their increasingly fluid lives (as well as working within the limitations of a mobile-phone display surface).

The P–C–E interaction

So, as we can see, understanding the dynamic interaction between Product–Consumer–Environment helps drive our understanding of the Brand Challenge, which stimulates the creation of the Idea ("the unexpected combination of previously unconnected thoughts"), which is then delivered through an unlimited number of points of contact.

The currency of Insight

Discovery has an end-point and that destination is "Insight".

"Insight" is the most overused and least understood word in marketing. Classically, people think of Insights as being "consumer insights" or "category insights", which give them inputs which they can play back to the consumer to demonstrate their understanding of the world. Traditionally, these are nothing more than narrow observations about product usage, gleaned from the usual sources of focus group and desk research. They are not true *Insights*.

Many companies have their own "processes" to unearth "insights". The problem is that, most of the time, Insights are things we stumble across, rather than carefully excavate.

Insight and intuition

Getting Insights is not stimulated by process. They are stimulated by triggers: an apple falling on your head, or moldy bread. (These "accidents" stimulated major scientific discoveries: the Law of Gravity, Penicillin.)

From Jesus Christ to Confucius, almost every great religious teacher or philosopher in the world has bemoaned the fact that most people can "see" but not understand. This is a good starting point. The dictionary defines "insight" as "the ability to see and understand clearly the inner nature of things, especially by intuition".

The key word here is "intuition". Intuition can be defined as "the direct knowing or learning of something without conscious reasoning". Letting go of reasoning is one of the hardest things we are asked to do in our jobs. Reason is our "comfort zone". It tells us where we are, and where we want to go. But it is not very good at helping us understand *how* to get there.

Did Dick Fosbury set a world record in the high jump through reason? He did the unthinkable: jumping headfirst and backwards over the bar! Before Jimi Hendrix we all naturally assumed the term "music" implied harmonies. No reasonable man would have doubted that. Jimi Hendrix was not a reasonable man!

Insights are about finding triggers rather than following a process; about output, not input; about using intuition rather than being a slave to reason.

From seeing to understanding

Insight is the difference between seeing and understanding. An Insight helps define the course of an action. It helps us reshape

the way people see their world; re-invent or re-interpret the
benefit of a product; reframe the brand ambition; and re-ignite
interest in a tired brand or category.

Let us illustrate each of these in turn:

- **How do we "reshape the way people see their world"?**
  Here we are really trying to get a handle on the beliefs,
  values or rituals that people share, which are unique to them
  as a group or "tribe". These are not directly related to the
  category or brand, but are made related, later, by the creative
  team.

  *In rural Thailand, institutional authority is regarded with
  disdain. The army and police force are routinely ridiculed in the local
  bars and clubs for their incompetence, corruption and cronyism. This,
  in turn, leads people to an acute sense of self-dependence when it comes
  to law and order.*

  *Now, armed with this Insight, if you were the creative team selling
  Mitsubishi tractors to farmers what would you do?*

  *Surely, you too would create a "superfarmer" character who
  rescues the beauty queen from the scoundrel kidnapper, under the noses
  of an absurdly incompetent squad of soldiers. Law and order can be
  achieved, with a little help from your friends!*

- **How do we "re-invent or re-inforce a product benefit"?**
  Here we are searching for ways to present the product
  benefit in a surprising way, so that the consumer sees the
  benefit in a different light. The way to do this is to interrogate
  the benefit until it confesses its weaknesses, then do
  something about it.

  *In India, Asian Paints is a brand of household paint. Paint
  brightens up homes everywhere. The quality of your home signifies
  your quality of life. The problem is, paint has a habit of getting
  everywhere. However, in India, "overflowing milk" symbolizes festivity,
  life and plenitude.*

India is also a country with a rich cultural heritage for bright colors. By combining these two observations, Asian Paints was able to position itself as a source of prosperity and a cause for celebration.

- **How do we "reframe the brand ambition"?**
Here we identify a problem that is stopping the brand growing. It is almost always unwise to tackle such problems head on. An Insight into the problem normally entails finding a way to outmaneuvre the problem by illustrating an alternative and superior "solution".

Across Asia, the overseas Chinese use traditional Chinese medicine (TCM) to improve their quality of life. This is a problem for the WWF's animal conservation program.

As 1997 was the Year of the Tiger, the WWF wanted a campaign to support tiger conservation. In Chinese tradition, certain tiger parts are supposed to increase sexual potency.

For years, the WWF had been trying to point out the futility of pushing tigers and other animal species towards extinction for the unproven (or even non-medical) benefits of TCM. It had little impact. In Chinese culture, even small improvements in human life are more valued than sparing animal life.

Clearly, the conservation effort could not work by competing with traditional culture. So, (just as a wrestler throws an opponent off balance by using his own weight against him) the agency switched approach, and decided to work with the logic of traditional culture.

Another part of Chinese tradition is the symbolic protection that tigers (and other animals) give to young children. Chinese men are also fathers. So, we outmaneuvered them <u>with</u> the new logic: if a species becomes extinct, it will not be able to offer the same "protection" to your children (and thus to the continuation of your sacred traditions).

- **How do we "re-ignite interest in the category or brand"?**
Here we might be able to change the nature of the brand to increase its appeal. To do this successfully, we should

manipulate what already exists in the consumer's mind, and encourage him/her to make new connections with the category or brand.

In Japan, Nissin Foods knows that instant noodles are never going to be the tastiest meals on the planet. They are a hole-filler for when you are hungry; and other snacking products can perform the same function equally well.

A few years ago, facing a host of alternative snack offerings, the instant noodles category came under the microscope. A simple, but brilliant, question triggered a big Insight: what does it really mean to be hungry?

In the context of the plight of millions who face starvation, it is genuinely a matter of "survival". But in an affluent culture where noodles play such a staple role in people's diet, to identify the brand with this far bigger "war on want" idea has made sure that both the brand and category survive.

Discover the blindingly obvious

The nature of Insights and how to get them is a far more complex subject than we can hope to do justice to in a single chapter. One piece of advice we would give to anyone in search of big Insights is to keep asking the question "Why?" until something so blindingly obvious emerges that you wonder why you haven't thought of it before.

Then, you will see and understand. As Shelly Lazarus, Chairman of Ogilvy & Mather Worldwide, has noted: "The test of a true Insight is that it is obvious in hindsight."

The following case study from India shows how comparing the use of refrigeration across different cultures provided a very useful Insight for the brand team.

CASE STUDY 5

Kelvinator refrigerators (India) — The Coolest One

Background

The Kelvinator refrigerator brand had enjoyed dominant status in the Indian marketplace until around 1992, with a 22% market share. However, due to a major strike and uncertainty over ownership of the brand, it fell to 6% by 1997.

Several factors were at play here — a factory strike had crippled output; the brand had been "loaned" to Whirlpool for a couple of years in the mid '90s; there had been significant under-investment in brand marketing; and new brands from multinational corporations had entered the marketplace.

Electrolux re-launched the Kelvinator brand in 1997. As part of the turnaround effort for the brand, the company approached Ogilvy.

The objective

The objective was to nurse the brand back to health, to arrest decline and set it back on track for growth.

The problems

Ogilvy's analysis of the brand's six core equities highlighted a number of key issues:

- **Image Equity** — This was a huge problem. The brand was well known but out of touch with changed consumer preferences.
- **Channel Equity** — Due to the confused ownership of the brand and other factors, the brand enjoyed little trade support, and had very poor distribution and in-store visibility.
- **Product Equity** — The brand had not found a differentiating point on which to compete. The product range was limited and there were no Frost Free models.

Overall, there was an urgent need for Insight. By finding a strong point of differentiation, 360 Degree marketing activities could begin to address the key image issues, and take solutions through the mix all the way to the store floor. But all this depended on finding a true Insight.

The breakthrough Insight

The brand team began by looking at the generic role of refrigeration and how the new players, the multinational brands, positioned themselves through marketing.

This, they discovered, was extremely Western-oriented, where refrigerators were used for storage and to keep foodstuffs fresher for longer.

This team then came across a breakthrough Insight. Fresh food is a daily habit for Indians, entailing daily trips to the neighborhood markets for many women. Keeping food fresh was not a priority for Indian women since they were going to buy fresh food the next day anyway. Closer analysis of Indian households, through observation and discussion with ordinary consumers, revealed a true Insight for Kelvinator. Most Indians needed a fridge for "cooling", not for "storage".

So it was on this Insight that Ogilvy built the brand campaign to revitalize the brand. The creative idea was "Kelvinator cools beyond the expected". And, it was decided that "The Coolest One" tagline was to be retained and strengthened with some cut-through creative work.

This revitalization process was aided by a concerted effort in the market with improved distribution, better trade relations and, most importantly, with the launch of a range of new models.

The Challenge

The Challenge was to create an indelible link between the brand and the benefit of rapid cooling, by taking it way beyond people's expectations.

Kelvinator Dentures · Point of Sale Item

Unusual point-of-sale material (chattering teeth!) reminded buyers that Kelvinator was definitely "the coolest one"

The Work

Television formed the spine of the campaign, with an amusing and arresting set of ads.

The press work built on this, talking about the features of the Kelvinator fridges and the things that were driving this amazing ability to make things cold — the most powerful compressor, the thickest insulation and the fastest ice-making facility.

Outdoor ads warned of the consequences of the revitalized brand: "12 months of Chill", "Summer? What Summer?", "Pull out your sweaters..."

A traveling rural roadshow, complete with a truck full of fridges, took the brand to the rural interior of India.

But, most importantly, the brand took the campaign in-store with prominent point-of-sale material that aggressively assured browsing customers that nothing cooled faster than "The Coolest One" — Kelvinator.

The Results

Kelvinator grew by 46% in 1999, with a share gain to 19%. And, despite a market slump in 2000, the brand continued to grow — a clear case of how Insight can lead to profit.

SAFE SEX AND THAILAND'S ELEPHANTS

"Our approach has not been conventional," says Dr Mechai Viravaidya, Secretary-General of Thailand's Population and Community Development Association. "In terms of providing information about safe sex, there must be many ways, not just the traditional ways." Spoken like a true 360 Degree brand evangelist.

Thailand's "Condom Campaign" is justifiably famous. Not only has it been highly effective, it set out to do what many commercial brands fail to do — namely, to find the most effective medium to reach its target audience, even if that medium is not one of the conventional formulas.

T-shirts, taxi cabs, and children's songs are just some of the innovative ways in which the family-planning message has been spread for AIDS prevention in Thailand. Perhaps the most famous, though, is a Bangkok restaurant called Cabbages and Condoms: "It's the only restaurant in the world where you can eat and get contraceptives at the same time," says Dr Mechai.

At a recent international conference on AIDS (where he handed out condom key chains to anyone within reach) Dr Mechai stressed the need for AIDS education in Thailand. Although many Thais are worried about AIDS, they know relatively little about it. But the spread of family planning has produced a model 360 Degree brand-awareness campaign. Over the course of four years, a network of community-based workers has been established in 16,000 villages. Contraceptives are now readily available. T-shirts display a modified portrait of the Mona Lisa, condoms in hand. Furthermore, it has sought to begin education at an early age. This has meant working with primary school children, getting them to blow up condoms instead of balloons so that they grow up to be adults

Elephants never forget. Nor should you.

who are not embarrassed by a simple device that should be worn by half the world's population. Alphabet songs and posters have also be adapted to educate — B for Birth, C for Condom etc.

But the most culturally unique media used in this campaign were a team of Thailand's indigenous elephants. For many years a common sight in Bangkok, elephants have in the past been used as giant billboards for various purposes (although the government has now set about getting them out of the city and back to their homes up north).

The Condom Campaign, however, used the elephants in the villages as walking billboards, reminding villagers to "Think Big, Think Condom". A memorable sight indeed, no doubt, for those who witnessed it.

8

Brand Involvement is King

"Go on, touch me — I use EverSoft"
T-shirt for EverSoft "naturally soft skin" shower foam

Most of us are aware of five senses: sight, sound, smell, touch and taste. There is, of course, a "sixth sense" — we have all experienced it at some point.* And a seventh — common sense.

It has always been something of a mystery to us why brand marketers and many communications agencies feel obliged to restrict themselves to using just two of these — sight and sound. Perhaps lacking the seventh sense themselves, they too easily overlook the opportunities to bring their brands alive for consumers in more meaningful ways by using more tangible sensory stimuli.

You will need little reminding at this stage that branding is not simply about advertising. It also extends beyond traditional marketing communications channels. There are a myriad

---

* In fact, the "sixth sense" also has a precedent in science — fish literally have one. It is called the "lateral-line" system, and consists of chains of nerve cells that extend along the body and in a scattering around the head. These nerve cells have small hairs that bend as water passes over them. This bending then triggers the cells to transmit electrical signals, allowing the fish to sense pressure changes, and detect exactly where their prey, or predators, are.

potential points of contact between a brand and its target consumer. If you limit yourself to trying to influence one or possibly two of these (TV advertising and direct mail, for instance), you are constricting the brand experience to a fraction of what it could be and are leaving the quality of the brand experience to factors outside your control.

360 Degree brand communications is not merely about delivering a message. It is about creating an experience of the brand through every potential point of contact with a consumer. The more senses you can activate, the more meaningful and intense that experience will be.

This chapter is not about product trial. It is about activating a brand experience via the sensory surround. To make this difference clear, we need to clarify exactly what we mean by "experience", and to distinguish clearly between the "product experience" and the "brand experience" — two interrelated but different things. (A quick illustration — assume you have never owned either a BMW car or an Apple computer. Now if your neighbor trades up to a BMW, does that not influence your opinion of the brand? If your best friend buys an i-Pod, does that not alter your relationship with Apple?)

The product experience

It is generally held to be true that, when stimulating trial for a product or service, one of the roles of advertising is to overcome the time lag between brand awareness and product experience. By demonstrating the product or service in action, or by having an existing user endorse it through a testimonial, or by comparing it to another similar product, you can build a pre-existing experience into the purchase. By the time the new user comes to actually buy your product, they will have "used" it mentally many times already, and will certainly be assured of its efficacy. It is for this reason they say that "nothing kills a bad product quicker than good advertising".

Of course, a product is all about this "real experience" — the ultimate experience of in-home use. Does the product deliver on its claims? Is it safe? Is it convenient and simple? Are there any design flaws? If there's any failure at this point, you can say goodbye to any repeat purchase. No amount of advertising can overcome a poor product experience.

However, these days there is a fundamental problem with basing brand communications on dramatizing a product experience — the "product experiences" of most brands in any given category are becoming indistinguishable from one another.

Differentiation is dead

As Robert Jones articulates in *The Big Idea*, there has been an explosion in two important dimensions over the past 20 years — choice and quality. "We live in a world of choice, of availability, on a scale never before seen," he says. And these choices are driving quality standards higher and higher; cars are increasingly reliable; good customer service is becoming a norm. And it's all being driven by competition. "In today's economy, more than ever, if you don't create a better deal for your customer, someone else will," Jones says.

Competition has created exponential choice, and enhanced quality. But, as Jones goes on to point out, "as products and services become better and better, they also become increasingly similar" — a development he calls "the blight of sameness".

According to research in the U.S., consumers believe that nearly 80% of all products in any particular category "offer the same thing" — meaning that you're kidding yourself if you really think your product is any different from the competitor's. It doesn't matter if it is or it isn't; the point is that consumers don't see it that way. They perceive parity everywhere.

This means we are witnessing the death of differentiation as a key sales driver. It has been shown in numerous studies that differentiation is the key engine behind brand growth. This is certainly true. But, most of the time, it is not *product* differentiation that is the engine of growth. For example, in China, we understand it takes on average a mere few weeks for a new technology to be understood, replicated, produced and got to market. Software is faster still. In the case of movies, the VCD is generally available on the streets of Shanghai before the première in London has even been concluded and the champagne served.

This means that the only form of sustainable differentiation available today is *brand* differentiation — creating a distinct emotion-based property and value-set that makes your range of products and services stand out from the crowd. More and more, the purchase decision is being driven by emotional decisions — how consumers *feel* about the brands they need to choose between — and not by functional differentiation.

The brand experience

So, if one of the key purchase discriminators is now a "feeling", a brand is thus obligated to create forms of advertising that not just impart information, but offer its customers an *experience* — and one that gives them something to feel about.

As a result, the brand is becoming an ever-more complex being; it is no longer sufficient to see it as simply the intangible sum of its parts. It has a life, a personality and a separate existence that forms the basis of a relationship with a consumer. Brands are complex, and they are becoming increasingly difficult to control — after all, brands only exist because of what the consumer *adds* to the product in his or her mind. As screen goddess Sophia Loren once said, "Sex appeal is 50% what you've got, and 50% what people *think* you've got."

Brand marketing these days is much more about trying to influence that second 50%, rather than reassuring consumers about the first. The modern Asian consumer is not a moron — she is a sophisticated, discriminating shopper, and she doesn't need to be told that a laundry detergent is good at cleaning clothes, or that an insect repellant kills effectively. Most of the brands on the shelf in front of her all clean or kill efficiently and effectively. If we want to create brand differentiation, if we want to influence her brand choice, we are going to have to make her *feel* something about our brand.

Creating a genuine, multi-faceted 360 Degree brand experience is also the only way of retaining control over brand perceptions in an increasingly fragmented world. The old-fashioned notion (which seems endearing to us now) of a simplistic binary relationship between a product and its advertising, between an effect and a single cause, between a purchase and a bit of long copy, cannot be sustained.

In a parallel universe to the actual product experience, the *brand experience* must now continue to deliver a level of engagement and interest that sustains consumers' interest, and involves them in an ongoing relationship. And it is only by approaching brand marketing from an altogether new, holistic perspective that a brand manager can hope to deliver a stimulating brand experience across a wide spectrum of contact points. 360 Degree communications strives to create an *experience* of the brand through every point of contact a customer has with that brand — and not simply to deliver a rational message.

The "Experience Economy"

There is a recent school of thought (most famously articulated by Joseph Pine and James Gilmore in their 1998 classic *The Experience Economy*) that suggests that the global economy is shifting from a service-led information economy, to an experiential event-based economy, where individuals are engaged in a personal experience by brands and services.

Over the past 200 years, the primary economic driver has moved from the extraction of commodities (essentially the farming and gathering of basic materials that are traded on the basis of supply and demand — coffee, oil, sugar) to the production of manufactured goods (made from raw materials, and sold according to product features) to, more recently, the provision of services (intangible and customized offerings that deliver benefits to customers).

In 1700, 80% of the U.S. workforce worked on farms; right now, 80% work in the "service economy". But that too is set to change. Because services are increasingly becoming commoditized — undifferentiated offerings that compete on price — it is only those services (or brands) that are creating memorable experiences for their customers who are able to sustain a price premium which are able to offer the consumer meaningful differentiation.

Pine and Gilmore use the example of the humble coffee bean. As a commodity, it fetches a few cents a cup. As a ground, ready-to-brew "good", it sells for about 10 cents a cup. Buying the "service" of a brewed cup of coffee in a regular café takes the price up to about 75 cents a cup. Yet many people are prepared to pay up to $5 a cup in a high-end espresso bar, where the heightened ambience and drama of the purchase creates an *experience*. The brand experience, in effect, is responsible for a massive price premium above the original commodity.

Brands are part of this move to the "experience economy". In the face of eroded differentiation, they need to move away from benefit-driven services to offer experiences that are both memorable and personal. Experiences need not be entirely about entertainment, but they must, at the very least, engage their targets.

Involvement

To create brand experiences that work, we need to find the right time, the right place, the right behavior and the right attitude of mind to engage the brand in the lives of its customers; in other words, we need to enhance "involvement".

Involvement is spoken of much and understood little,

especially by single-discipline "experts". We like to think of involvement as something a little more sophisticated than just art-direction or the choice of some incidental music to go with the pictures. To us, true involvement is what is created by increasing the pitch on two important dimensions — **intensity** (making a brand experience more memorable), and **interplay** (using different points of contact to amplify the overall brand experience).

These two dimensions are at the heart of creating an involving brand experience.

Interplay — creating resonance

This requires a full and detailed understanding of the consumer's "world" — how the brand and your target consumer's life do and can intersect. Locating these potential "encounter points" allows a brand to orchestrate the interaction between them in order to amplify the message/experience.

This approach to interplay has a profound effect on media channel selection. Finding the right media to put a brand experience in front of a consumer at the right moment is as creative an arena as the idea-generation itself. Points of contact come in all sorts of different shapes and sizes: a park bench, a convex mirror, a staircase, a pager, tattoos, a potted plant, and even a wine cork have all been used as media. Media planners need to understand that they have a role as "creative directors" too — new media are not selected, they are created. For a more detailed discussion about creating interplay, fast-forward to the next chapter.

Intensity — dramatizing a brand experience

This requires a full and detailed understanding of what the *right* experience is for a brand to create. It requires finding the right context to bring that experience to life, and then using the full sensory possibilities to intensify it.

Intensification is only possible if you have a clear impression of the type of experience your brand should be trying to create. One way to know this is to imagine the perfect type of world your brand ought to inhabit.

Here are some examples of these "imaginary worlds" from the minds of some consumers we interviewed. A "Mercedes-Benz world" would be one in which nothing ever breaks down; where the engineering excellence is so high that doors open without a squeak; trains arrive perfectly on time; everyone is perfectly dressed in understated designer suits. Volvo lives in a world where people feel invulnerable; where commuters skydive to work; a world where adventure is maximized and risk minimized. Singapore Airlines occupies a world where service is impeccable; and where every whim is catered for. And Nokia is a world where people are telepathic; where there is total connection between everyone; no loneliness; and a powerful sense of community.

Having heard them paint these kinds of mental pictures, it is easier to see how to bring this imaginary brand world alive as an experience for real consumers in real time, through as many points of contact as possible.

This sort of "idea-intensification" exercise leads directly to a new kind of media planning, where in place of titles, programs and schedules, we could have a series of *experiences*. Of course, experiences require relevant and affordable communications channels to make a brand "world" real and to intensify our target consumer's experience of that brand. But understanding how channel planning can create involvement for a brand through *experiences* could radically change the emphases on which types of communication these brands might engage in, and may re-prioritize marketing budgets according to such things as "intensity", "depth of involvement", "interplay contribution" and "range of engagement" instead of good old "reach and frequency".

Adding value to brand communications

"Our ability to surround the consumer with the brand in ways that work effectively increases the value of what we offer exponentially." So says Shelly Lazarus, Chairman of Ogilvy & Mather Worldwide. Brand involvement is not for fun: it is, at heart, a business and a marketing proposition that aims to provide better sales, increased market share and a higher return on investment.

Bringing the brand experience to a wider range of contact points, enhancing involvement, increasing the intensity and interplay of these ideas, all add to the efficiency of brand communications. Each point of contact builds the experience in a way that far surpasses the impact of using one traditional channel alone. This ultimately represents a dollar saving, since the quality of the brand impression is that much higher than that produced by traditional approaches, and thereby a more efficient way of building brand messaging.

Secondly, various studies by research companies such as Millward Brown (a research and information consultancy and part of WPP) have shown that the one truly reliable indicator of future sales is "involvement". Not "spontaneous awareness", not "enjoyability", nor even "comprehension", but *brand involvement* — the very thing that's produced by a combination of the intensity of the brand experience and the interplay between those experiences.

Practical implications

So what are the practical implications of all this for brand communications and marketing?

Firstly, to expect to create, maintain, enhance and update a "brand relationship" using only a single, passive-consumption medium like TV is both naïve and unrealistic. Even adding secondary and tertiary media, such as print or outdoor, only *begins* the job of creating a brand experience — it raises awareness, of course, but is also raises expectations. What else? What next? The consumers' appetite for fulfillment has increased. They expect more from a brand.

Obviously, an advertising idea alone cannot build a brand experience. Here are some of the ways different disciplines might set about creating different types of experience.

Immersion Marketing — in the action

Immersion techniques seek to take the brand experience actively to the consumers, rather than passively parading it in front of them. The increasing tendency of the consumer to avoid being sold to — the so-called "sophisticated consumer" with a finely tuned marketing radar — has made radar-busting techniques an important part of the marketing armory.

(Reproduced with kind permission of RedCard)

By combining an understanding of the cynicism of being sold to on the one hand, with their desire to be engaged and entertained on the other, Immersion Marketing seeks out media combinations that aim to interact with consumers, in a way that fuses intelligence and wit with a sense of daring and panache. On-street or in-store are the favored "reality marketing" venues for immersive brand experiences, which tend to confront or seduce, rather than persuade or inform. These range from laser-projections on buildings and street-painting on sidewalks, to giving free rickshaw rides round town to get busy executives to and from lunch meetings for *The Economist*, to swarms of KFC "assassins" carrying out brand stunts in high-traffic fast-food areas, to providing "boyfriend crèches" for Motorola in shopping malls at weekends.

Sales Promotion — branding the "last mile"

Traditionally, clients have two budgets — a marketing budget that pays for all brand development activities, from advertising to public relations to the point-of-sale collateral; and a trade budget which is used to pay retailers for listing fees, display features and in-store promotions. In most cases, these budgets are treated very separately, and sometimes even handled by different departments. The net result of this is that the investment made in creating brand equity stops at the door of the retailer. Brand development happens *outside* the store. Sales take place inside.

This misses a crucial point; namely, that the key moment in a brand's existence — the "point of decision", the culmination of the entire branding effort — is entirely ignored by brand marketers and advertisers alike. This represents a major opportunity for the Sales Promotion agency — to be able to "brand the last mile" and take the brand experience all the way to the point of purchase.

By understanding what the influences are that might shape the time, the place, the behavior and the attitudes of the consumer at the very point of decision, communications techniques can extend the brand experience to the very "moment of truth", when a consumer makes a decision to buy one brand over another. Traditional brand marketing leaves that moment alone, hoping that the residual weight of all previous brand activity will be sufficiently memorable to sway a decision once in store. 360 Degree brand communications says that that moment is too important not to be a crucial focus for reinforcing a brand experience.

The Interactive Experience — entertain or die

Nothing exemplifies the need for a brand experience better than the online world. "Stickiness" was one of the buzz words of year 2000. A site which didn't have it was doomed — as one ad at the time (for a brand that has long since disappeared) rather ominously reminded us (against the backdrop of a towering Hawaiian wave), "four out of five surfers never return". If the brand fails to offer a relevant experience for the visitor, there is no incentive or reason for them to come back.

The experience of the brand online could take several directions — it could offer information, or entertainment, or a sense of community, or a combination of all three. Either way, unless the brand is adding significant value to the experience of being on that site at that moment, it is both inefficient and irrelevant.

Conversely, from a brand's perspective, the web offers an excellent and innovative space to create or extend a brand experience. Many brands have worried about having a reason for going online; to our mind, there is no better reason than supplying a relevant, "sticky" and involving experience to engage the consumer and *extend* the brand experience into the virtual world.

Public Relations — influencing the experience

Brand experiences don't have to be conscious "in your face" confrontations — guerilla solutions are not for everyone. For example, a brand's reputation is one of the most important factors in how a consumer *feels* about a brand, and yet influencing brand reputation is a more subtle, more sophisticated and a longer-term exercise than some of the above examples might indicate. Within a 360 Degree context, it is an experience largely controlled by the Public Relations agency or the Brand Identity company.

Customers (and their purchasing habits) are increasingly influenced by how they think and feel towards the companies that produce the brands and services on offer. We know that customers are more loyal to reputable brands. We also know they will not pay a premium for the goods and services of a company they don't respect. And furthermore, if a brand has consistently been a strong part of the community it operates in, it will have built up goodwill that can influence a customer's perceptions positively, even in a crisis situation.

A brand's reputation amongst consumers is confirmed or enhanced (or damaged) mainly *outside* the traditional "advertising" media channels. A reputation gets made (for better or for worse) in editorial content, online reviews, by pundits and experts, on chat-shows and in chat-rooms, beside the watercooler, in the store, via employee behavior, and everywhere in between. At first glance, these may seem like difficult brand experiences to control. But they <u>can</u> be influenced.

If a company acts responsibly upstream, it goes a long way to influencing positively its reputation downstream. By "managing the messaging" as much as possible, a brand can wield a surprising level of control over its reputation and therefore the *brand experience* it offers.

A foreign firm entering a local market can appoint key, local influencers who are strongly aligned to the brand to endorse or even serve that brand; from being a hostile in-comer, the brand now offers the experience of a welcome and trusted local partner. Smaller companies can create alliances, which in turn improves their reputation by association; they go from being an unknown (and high-risk) nobody, to offering the experience of being trusted suppliers.

Brands which are serious about generating influence can also influence legislative or government decision-making processes; they now offer the experience of a brand which will champion and fight for just causes. And employees who really understand their company's brand make for extremely powerful advocates whose influence on reputation cannot be underestimated; a brand that is endorsed by its employees offers others a brand experience of integrity (which, by the way, provides yet another good reason to show why internal communications are now just as important as external, customer-focused communications, and an integral part of the 360 Degree brand plan).

Conclusion

All this goes to show how diverse the armory available is for brand owners to shape the experience they want to offer their consumers; and how blinkered an advertising-only brand campaign really is. Influencer-marketing, public relations, guerrilla "hits", ambient media, new media, internal communications, trade promotions, brand promotions, events, media relations, editorial context, sampling, sponsorship and viral conflagrations are all ways of bringing the brand experience to life. With seven senses to play with, it is not difficult for a brand to differentiate itself in new and refreshing ways. Simply relying on narrow-band visual messaging suddenly seems like a wasted opportunity and a rather boring, monochrome response to what is probably a dynamic and sophisticated marketing or business problem. Both you and your brand deserve more.

All this talk of "experiential marketing" has several implications for agencies:

- the traditional narrowband "ad agency" needs to fill out its ability to deliver a totally integrated response to marketing problems. This functionality can either exist in-house or via affiliations and partnerships, so long as it is properly integrated and not just "briefed in".

- the "brand idea" needs to triumph over the one-track "executional idea". No longer can the 30-second TV spot dictate the tone, content, talent, style, imagery for a fully rounded marketing communications package. Roll over, prima donnas: idea-generation has become the obligation of the entire team, not just a couple of individuals.

- executional ideas can be anything. Suddenly, a brand medium could be a T-shirt, a soundtrack, an event, a promotion, a sponsorship, a balloon, a direct-mail piece or an endorsement from someone you respect or know ... anything is possible, so long as it is both consistent with the brand and offers a practical solution to that Brand Challenge.

Let's look at how one brand set about creating a total *brand* experience, rather than simply relying on a *product* experience (however good).

CASE STUDY 6

Left Bank Café (Taiwan)

This case illustrates how the marketing and agency teams were forced to think creatively and laterally in establishing a new brand of coffee in Taiwan and in bringing the entire "brand experience" to the target in fresh and innovative ways. Uniquely, this project began with the agency helping to invent and then create the actual "product experience" as well.

Background

In 1997, President Foods Ltd., a large Taiwanese packaged-goods manufacturer, had a superior refrigeration and distribution system for selling cold drinks through convenience stores. In Taiwan, the nature of the packaging determines the retail selling price to a far greater degree than the cost of making the drinks it contains. Thus a beverage sold in a tetra-pak, regardless of whether it contains a high-cost coffee or a low-cost soya milk, always retails at NT$10–15. And any beverage that comes in a can is always sold at NT$20.

President Foods wanted to sell the same kinds of beverages, but in a packaging that would allow for a price point of NT$25. And so it developed a plastic cup. This would signal to the consumer that the contents were fresh, and the consumer was prepared to pay more for fresh drinks. At this point, the agency (Ogilvy & Mather Taiwan) was asked to get involved. Of the various options tested, fresh coffee was found to have the most premium image. But there were many ready-to-drink coffee brands — parity was already built into this market. Differentiation, as with so many other categories in so many other markets, needed to be because of brand, and brand experience.

Premium values were researched and tested, and the result was a decision to create a brand that leveraged the values of coffee from Paris — from a café on the Left Bank of the Seine, a place full of atmosphere, a haunt of poets and philosophers.

The emotive appeal of the Parisian Left Bank was huge amongst the heaviest users of ready-to-drink coffee — city-dwelling young women aged 17–22. Honest, sentimental, full of hopes and dreams, and fond of art and literature, they looked for much more from a brand than simply a functional product experience. They were searching for things (and brands) that made them feel more sophisticated.

Making the consumer feel part of the French Left Bank experience

The Challenge

In concept form, the brand was a potent one. However, the larger Brand Challenge facing the agency team was how to make the brand as sophisticated and artistic in real life as it was on paper, or in the dreams of their focus-group respondents.

The TV advertising that had been developed encouraged people to build in their own minds a picture of this favorite French café. A series of print ads told little tales of things that had happened in the café, as seen through the eyes of the waiters. Poetic vignettes were broadcast as radio ads.

But this alone was not enough — the target had mostly never been to Paris or even seen a French café. The key insight for developing 360 Degree communications was that the brand was not selling coffee at all, but a café. The brand needed to deliver its experience as a tangible reality.

Three French waiters helping to bring the Left Bank Café to life

The Work

First, the agency organized a photographic exhibition of Parisian café life at Taiwan's biggest bookstore. Simultaneously, it decided to open a real (but temporary) café on the pavement outside, on the basis that the novelty of the café would both attract media interest and pull people into the photographic exhibition inside.

Ogilvy Public Relations secured agreement for this from Taipei council, and arranged media coverage. O&M Advertising, in conjunction with Mindshare (a fellow WPP media "planning and buying" agency) and the French Council, then arranged for the development of a cable-TV program about French cafés called "The Left Bank Café Tour", which introduced 20 Parisian cafés as well as a certain temporary one on the streets of Taipei.

Next, the Left Bank Café brand helped the French Institute organize a film festival around French National Day, bringing in co-sponsors Renault, Peugeot, Chanel, Dior and, of course, the one brand you will never find in France — Left Bank Café.

The success of all this activity was tangible. So successful was the brand team in creating a living, breathing brand experience that a staggering 80% of young women interviewed actually believed that Left Bank Café really existed in Paris, and that it would soon open a branch in Taiwan. As one interviewee put it: "Does Left Bank Café really exist? I prefer to believe in a world where it does."

The second phase of this campaign developed the theme one stage further. If initially the brand experience had taken people to Paris in their imaginations, now it was time to take them to Paris in real life, and brand the entire experience as Left Bank Café. What looked like a promotional idea on the surface was actually a complex piece of 360 Degree brand magic.

Eva Air's daily flight to Paris was branded Left Bank Café. Via a sales promotion competition, winners were found, issued with tickets and brought to the airport. All passengers on the flight were handed back their travel documents with a Left Bank travel wallet that included a café guide to Paris. Left Bank coffee was served in the departure lounge. The on-board welcome speech was made first in French and then in Chinese. French movies were screened, as well as the TV guide to café life in Paris. Headrests, pillow cases, table mats, meal trays, paper cups and the cabin decoration took on Left Bank branding.

Helping turn a plastic cup into a brand
(Reproduced with kind permission of
President Foods Taiwan)

The Results

The promotion was launched to the wider public via the media. An on-board press conference with French waiters, mime artists and musicians kicked off the three-month campaign, which has since led to a queue of other organizations — from railways to travel agents to department stores — lining up to partner Left Bank in future "brand experience" initiatives.

By understanding both the brand and their consumer in great depth, the marketing and agency teams were able to breathe life into a premium brand that otherwise would have remained a two-dimensional concept in ad breaks and on the back page of magazines.

The lesson to be drawn from this is to see how much more powerful a brand property can be when it is *allowed to live as an experience*, to occupy a sensory space, and literally reach out and touch its target consumer.

THE STAR FERRY IN HONG KONG

Hong Kong's Victoria Harbor is justifiably famous. Dramatically positioned between the high ridges that back Kowloon to the north and The Peak on Hong Kong Island to the south, and lined by that unique skyline of towering skyscrapers, the harbor is in constant motion. One of the busiest stretches of water in the world, the narrow gap between Kowloon and HK Island is bridged over 200 times a day by the distinctive Star Ferry.

First established in 1888, the Star Ferry has been running more or less continuously for 114 years, and always in its famous green-and-white livery. The Star Ferry is a true Hong Kong icon and is instantly recognizable to anyone who has ever been there. It is also a highly visible part of city life, carrying thousands of people every day from one side of the harbor to the other. In other words, it was a media vehicle waiting to happen.

Which is exactly how media agency OMD saw it. In 1999, they were looking for a big idea for their client, Virgin Atlantic, which was soon to launch its London-Shanghai route. The idea to brand the Star Ferry by painting the entire boat in the striking red and white of the Virgin colors first surfaced at a brainstorming session, only to be met with a fair degree of skepticism — entirely understandable, given the fact that the Star Ferry had never before been anything other than green and white.

Enthusiasm for the idea only kicked in once a persistent OMD found a large model of the Star Ferry and had it mocked-up into Virgin colors, complete with a massive logo on its topsides. From there, the idea went to the senior management of the Wharf Group, owners of the ferry, who gave it the go-ahead. And so came about one of the more famous "world's first" media ideas. It won *Media Magazine's* "Most Creative Use of Media" Award 1999, and gained worldwide recognition for both Virgin and OMD. Richard Branson loved it, of course.

For a very small cost, Virgin achieved huge amounts of awareness; not only through worldwide press coverage of the painted ferry, but also in HK, where the highly arresting red and white Star Ferry continued to ply its trade across the harbor in full view of residents and visitors alike for a whole six months. Even the official tourist authority, HKTA, used the Virgin Star Ferry in its own material, as it seemed to breathe new life into a famous HK icon.

The launch of the ferry was fused with a promotion called "The world's biggest offer" (another typical Virgin sideswipe at British Airways), in which Virgin Atlantic bought the whole of HK a free ride on the Star Ferry for an entire weekend.

Of course, the idea has been copied several times since by several other brands. But when it comes to media, being first is always important; the one people remember most is the one that does it first — the Virgin ferry — which simply underlines the need to turn original ideas into action. As Mike Cooper, CEO of OMD Asia-Pacific, says, "Having a unique media idea in the first place is only part of it — making it happen is the important thing. Seventy per cent of great ideas never even leave the room they are born in."

9

Creating Interplay

"There are no longer any boundaries to media. From SMS to videogames to product placement to digital communication, there are literally millions of permutations available to brand owners. Where on earth do they start?"
Mark Austin, CEO, MediaEdge:CIA Asia-Pacific

At the beginning of this chapter, we ought to apologize in advance. So far, we have tried to avoid too much technical or invented jargon. But, here we want to introduce three concepts that have emerged over time as we have practiced 360 Degree Branding®:

Sequencing and layering — identifying the optimum selection of media channels and points of contact to deliver the greatest degree of brand involvement

Idea intensification — looking for interplay between different points of contact to enhance the cumulative impact of the Brand Idea

Contextual creativity — finding executional ideas which fuse the message and medium, so that they work *as a combination* exclusively for that brand, at that time, in that place, for that audience.

This is the area where we need some highly creative media thinking. This is not a chapter about media planning or buying (there are whole textbooks devoted to that subject) but, rather, about creativity in media.

Sequencing and layering

At first glance, any media plan has a sequence that shows different layers in the campaign: often, a TV burst, followed by some print insertions, supplemented by a "tertiary" medium designed to ... (take your pick):

- extend coverage
- build frequency
- pick up a secondary audience
- test a different medium
- go into a supplementary region
- take advantage of, or flatten out, seasonality in sales
- avoid single-execution wear-out
- hero (or publicize) the campaign through its PR value
- support a non-advertising activity (e.g. a sales or trade promotion, or a community goodwill program)

All of these, and many others, can be laudable objectives. The point is that in all these instances the media-planning thinking is conducted independently of the Idea development. This is *not* 360 Degree thinking.

In determining the optimum sequencing and layering to create brand involvement, the first requirement is to frame the key objectives of the campaign. There are three basic objectives:

- to gain awareness (i.e. break through the clutter of competitor communications — raise share-of-mind)
- to create imagery (i.e. generate longer-term brand attributes by creating, changing or reinforcing an image)
- to make a sell (i.e. directly influence behavior, either via a trial purchase, or via more loyalty).

- **Gain awareness**
  The way you might frame your message, and use pack shots, signage, slogans, brand colors, icons or celebrities associated

with the brand can have a big impact here. You must ask yourself how you want to go about this.

Do you want to create a mnemonic, either to stimulate recall of the brand promise (perhaps in the manner of "Intel Inside" via the musical sting) or to improve brand recognition (in the manner of the Marlboro cowboy or the McDonald's arches)?

Do you need to create a link between the category and an unfulfilled need? You may want to remind people about a latent need they often forget about (drinking milk, for example), or to establish a need for a new kind of product that people are not familiar with (such as using a mobile Internet service).

- **Create imagery**

  People have relationships with brands that exist beyond the purely functional benefits they provide. Brands have personalities or attitudes that help people identify with and trust them. But, these brand attitudes take time and effort to create and nurture.

  If you want to alter the way people feel about your brand, do you want to create an attitude, where one did not exist previously (as happened, for example, when Nike asked us all to "Just Do It")? Do you want to increase the intensity of a strong positive (e.g. BMW or Sony)? Perhaps you want to maintain the attitude — it's perfect (as in Rolex or Singapore Airlines)? On the other hand, you may wish to modify the way people feel, from one positive to another (as in American Express's shift from "Don't leave home without it" to "Do more"). Or do you want to change people's attitude, replacing a negative with a positive? This may be a brand problem that needs emergency repair (for example, the "Tylenol murders"); or the brand has a very strong positive association that also carries negative baggage, which needs to be countered (for example, Volvo's link with "safety", making the cars seem boring).

- **Make a sell**

  "We sell, or else" was another popular refrain from our founder, David Ogilvy. All communications must create a sell. But they can do this in different ways.

  Do you want to encourage people to take immediate action — to recommend the brand for someone else to buy (kids' toys or perfume or insurance); to buy the brand for themselves at the next relevant opportunity (most fast-moving consumer goods); or to use the brand more, so they need to replace it quicker (photographic film, cooking sauces)?

  Do you need to do something more to stimulate purchase (make a price or giveaway offer to help overcome a barrier to purchase; make it easier for them to locate or search for the brand by mentioning dealerships, telephone hotlines, websites, home visits or whatever; devise a promotion, competition, or other offer)?

  The setting of objectives is not necessarily a linear process. Indeed, in a 360 Degree campaign, it is the Brand Idea that determines how the messaging is sequenced and layered through various executional ideas, in whatever discipline. Each executional idea should build the overall Brand Idea, by taking advantage of the specific strengths of that form of communication.

  Taking an analogy from farming, it is possible to think of sequencing and layering in terms of the following periods of cultivating the emotional bonding of consumers, as the campaign builds:

  Prepare the ground: raise prior awareness of the issues the brand will address. This makes the consumer attuned to the benefits, user imagery, attitudes/values or mission that will be at the core of the brand's positioning

  Plant the seeds: position the brand, particularly among influencers whose endorsement is vital to success, as providing the solution to the issues

Grow the plants: expand on the benefits, user imagery, attitudes/values, mission to get the message across powerfully

Protect the harvest: anticipate how to counter competitors who may attack the brand's new position

Improve the yield: develop new initiatives to take the brand into new categories and markets or create advocates of emotionally bonded users.

Idea intensification

An Idea is an Idea; there are no big ones or small ones, 360 Degree ones or other ones. The simple truth of creativity is that you have an Idea, then see where you can take it, and try (where possible) to deliver it at a level *beyond* people's expectations. As the painter Henri Matisse observed: *"An artist has but one idea. He is born with it, and spends a lifetime developing it and making it breathe."*

The point here is not to over-intellectualize how ideas emerge ("Are they the result of a little piece of magic? Or, a god-given right of only a few semi-mortal souls? The result of a sudden dose of inspiration? Only defined retrospectively?" etc). It doesn't really matter how the neural processes in the brain work. Once we have the germ of an Idea, then is the time to get to work to intensify the Idea until it *becomes* big.

It is a bit like "surround sound". Surround sound enriches the experience, but doesn't question or hamper the process of sound production.

Here we look for interplay between the various points of contact, and explore the diversity of options we have in those points of contact. (You will no doubt recall the number of different media that were used in the San Miguel Light campaign highlighted earlier, and how they all contributed to building up the very personality of the animated character, Sammy.) One way of stimulating your team to think about all the possible points of contact that could intensify the brand Idea is to probe hard on two dimensions: What is happening in people's lives? And, where could the brand intercept and involve them?

It requires a switch in the thinking process away from reach and frequency, impressions, hits, column inches and response rates, to a consideration of how the brand can become part of their lives at certain times and places, with certain behaviors and attitudes of mind — the morning commute, the coffee break, a lazy Saturday morning.

We need to ask more searching questions:

- What is happening in people's lives that might affect their relationship with the brand?
- Who or what do they specifically identify with in the world at large that the brand could pick up on?
- What is new in the marketplace that may influence the way they feel about the brand?
- When are the brand's consumers most involved in the media they consume?
- Is there a natural fit between the brand and its customers' lifestyles?
- What is changing in the way the brand's customers consume media?
- In what way could the use of media be tailored to intensify the relationship between different audiences?
- Is there a natural sequence to the choice or use of media in building greater involvement with the brand?

There is one rule in all this: Understand the complexity, then simplify.

Contextual creativity

"You can't use your judgment if your imagination is out of focus." so said author Mark Twain.

Searching questions lead to intriguing points of contact. Sometimes we are looking for a total fusion of message and medium, so that the one doesn't mean anything without the other, and vice versa.

Consider the target reader of *The Economist* in Asia. How do you involve, constantly and intelligently, an aspiring senior executive who is always on the move and on the way up the greasy corporate ladder? He is too busy to be exposed to traditional media. The brand has to be where he is in some down-time, even if this is only for a few seconds or so: getting out of the taxi on the way to a convention center, waiting at the platform for the airport express train, between the train and the check-in desk.

Airport Express Train, Hong Kong

Airport Express Station, Hong Kong

Skytrain in Bangkok

Chep Lap Kok Airport,
Hong Kong

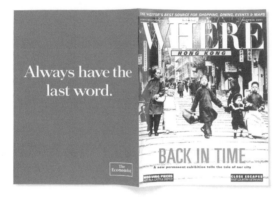

Back cover WHERE *magazine,*
Hong Kong

Magazine wrap cover

Caltex House, Singapore

Airport trolley

Blimp, somewhere over Asia!
(Reproduced with kind permission of
The Economist)

This is where you need ingenuity; real ingenuity. This is the preserve of the "Renaissance Man". People often repeat Marshall McLuhan's dictum that "the medium is the message"; but in 360 Degree Branding®, the medium and the message must also be totally integrated to be more than just a gimmick.

For example, one dot-com had the ingenious idea of advertising its website address on wine corks. Every time you opened a nice bottle of wine, there it was, looking at you right in the face. Compare this with the sticker on the apple that says, "I grew this apple especially for you — God".

The wine cork is a very creative, innovative and arresting choice of medium, but the apple works harder. It integrates the medium and the message in a way that makes you think, hard, about the meaning of life.

The following case study ably dramatizes the power and sophistication of a phased, 360 Degree media-planning schematic. By using the different media in an orchestrated fashion, it enhances the quality (and, therefore, the effectiveness) of the messaging, thereby increasing the efficiency of the overall media spend.

IBM e-Society (China): Sustaining IBM's e-Business leadership by strengthening the brand's connection with China

Background

In 1998, IBM in China was facing strong local competition, who were aggressively stealing share of voice and share of market. All the while, Internet penetration was growing apace and business use of technology was exploding.

Undaunted by this, IBM set itself a bold challenge — to capture the fast-growing market and become undisputed leader of the "new-paradigm China".

e-Business campaign

In one of the most successful campaigns ever undertaken, IBM globally stole the high ground by naming the paradigm itself (e-Business), a positioning it went on to own exclusively in (business) consumers' minds, thereby securing its own future as a company.

While still wishing to be perceived as an international company, IBM saw the opportunity to align itself with a society that was undergoing massive change and, in the process, rapidly emerging as a major adopter of technology.

IBM's strategy was to use "e-Society" as a complementary theme to its business-to-business campaign. Such an umbrella idea would allow for messaging that could embrace the entire universe of IBM product and service capability — technological leadership, hardware, software, solutions, services and applications.

"Share of mind" was the primary objective, but such a campaign would also convert to opportunities to generate demand.

Campaign overview

The IBM messages were carried to the people of China via press releases, print advertising and public service announcements, and outdoor media in Beijing and Chengdu. The campaign also made use of a range of interactive media — a web sitelet, flash banners, a screen saver and cursors — and intranet internal communications.

Phased media interplay

The media campaign was orchestrated in seven phases:

- **Phase One: Internal communications**

  The IBM China intranet was chosen to be the most suitable medium for communicating with all staff. As members of Chinese society themselves, they were a very important target audience. It was felt that the employees had the right to be the first to be exposed to this major new campaign. Their goodwill and buy-in was vital to get the program off to a flying start. At this point, the Ogilvy PR team launched the "e-IBM-er", an online employee communications vehicle designed to ensure that the entire IBM organization understood the company's new direction.

- **Phase Two: Engaging the brain**

  The next phase was to push out into print media low-branded content that discussed the transformation of Chinese society into an e-Society, probing the development from the concept to reality.

  The Public Relations team at Ogilvy leveraged third-party allies to help explain the transformation that was taking place within IBM, both worldwide and in China. This took the form of articles and editorials that appeared in quality magazines and newspapers and as "thought-pieces".

  Thus, even before what would traditionally be called the ad-campaign had started, the key "endline" (e-Society) was already gaining currency amongst journalists, commentators and business leaders.

- **Phase Three: Splashdown**

  The visually unique and arresting print campaign was launched in a big way. A four-page back-to-back section announced that e-Society was ready, that it was already a part of Chinese society and was supported by the government. It described how both enterprises and people's lives had been and would be changed in the e-Society.

  The campaign gave the Chinese a chance to look at their own culture objectively, in a fascinating new light, and generated a wealth of pride.

- **Phase Four: Awareness and imagery**

  The outdoor campaign, featuring bold and engaging black-and-white images, struck through with the dashing red of an e-shaped ampersand, turned heads and stuck in the mind.

  It echoed the print, and helped recognition and engagement for the later stage of the print campaign.

Web banner reinforcing the message that "e-Society" is now here

Posters announcing "The Birth" of e-Society in Beijing
(Reproduced with kind permission of IBM China)

- **Phase Five: The introduction of the enabler**
  The next wave of print ads finally elaborated on the IBM role in Chinese e-Society. It showed how the brand had been the instigator behind many of the technological developments in Chinese businesses. At the same time, the brand promised to forge ahead with China, to work alongside and with her business enterprises, both private and State-owned, by continuing to provide its world-class technology and talent (in products and services) to drive Chinese enterprise in the global marketplace. Again an aggressive round of Public Relations was employed at this point in the campaign.

- **Phase Six: Mass announcement**
  In the mind of the Chinese consumer, nothing and no-one could endorse such a campaign with more authority than the Chinese State. Therefore, in

a stroke of audacity, the brand team co-developed their TV campaign with CCTV, the national TV station, and turned advertising into a series of Public Service Announcements.

The spots publicized the speed of digitalization (a key agenda issue for the State) and also strengthened the brand's relationship with the Government itself.

They related various stories about how the e-Society was creating change and opportunity for ordinary people. Here's one such story:

"When I left college, my friends — one after the other — all started to leave China and go abroad. I lost 11 classmates in two years — eight to North America and three to Europe. I chose to stay in China, and do something here. I wanted to make a difference. Last year, I started a business. On the Web. It wasn't easy. But guess what? My friends are now coming home. To work with me."

China's e-Society: Success belongs to everyone.

- **Phase Seven: Sustaining a web presence**
  Finally, the obvious place for an e-campaign saw the development of websites and interactive banners and down-loadables. These served as long-term interfaces for the brand and the curious consumer.

  The sites support the advertising and help consumers better understand the changes they are living through, the e-Society and IBM's role within that.

Conclusion

By viewing the campaign development phase by phase, it is clear to see how the message was intensified by sequencing and building. While not complex, its superiority over the tradition cyclical waves/bursts of activities (all going at once) is obvious to us all. Media interplay in a 360 Degree context can be and ought to be an integral part of generating the Brand Idea.

PUPPET SHOWS IN INDONESIA

Indonesia is a vast country, comprising over 14,000 different islands (of which "only" 930 are inhabited). It is the world's fourth-most-populous country, with 200 million inhabitants (over 30% of whom are under 15). And it is a veritable mosaic of different ethnic groups and cultures, with dozens of different languages.

These three basic facts make Indonesia an extremely difficult consumer market to manage — its sheer size and diversity mean that relying on standard media communications methods is not an option. Marketing in Indonesia more often than not means *taking the message and the brand directly to the consumer.* An example of how this is being done is the use of *wayang kulit,* traditional Indonesian puppet theater.

Wayang is a Javanese word meaning "shadow" or "ghost" and refers to a theatrical performance using the shadow images of two-dimensional puppets projected before a backlit screen (*wayang kulit*). The performance is controlled by the *dalang* (the puppeteer), who manipulates the puppets, sings, signals to the orchestra, and speaks the parts for all the characters — a true Account man!

Mostly found in Java, it represents one of the oldest continuous traditions of storytelling in the world, and is one of the most highly developed. It is also thoroughly integrated into Javanese society. Therefore, it is perfectly suited to becoming a medium for telling *brand* stories.

A typical wayang puppet in Indonesia.

Such shadow plays are traditionally performed in villages and towns on public holidays, religious festivals, weddings, birth celebrations and circumcisions. They form part of a tradition of bringing people together to tell stories and impart information.

Therefore, more recently, brands have found it a natural way to bring together an audience, and tell them a brand story. Almost like a "road show" for brands that also involves cultural performances by local artistes, these performances fuse *wayang* with a product story woven into the fabric of the folklore. Immediately following the performances, the audience is treated to product demonstrations and/or sampling.

10

Collaborative Partnerships — the Spirit of Cross-Discipline Integration

"Two heads are better than one."
The Hydra — mythical, multi-headed creature

Theory is all well and good. It looks nice on paper, in training manuals and in books like these. But it is nothing without implementation, without human structures and teams who understand the ideas and can deliver solutions based on those ideas.

360 Degree brand communication demands a new and different way of working. Old-style integration agencies may not even be sitting in the same buildings as their sister companies, and may still be operating as separately as competitors. But simply coming together physically will not produce miracles. It is easy to forget that the human element, the blending and building of working teams and practices, is a highly important part of the development of big, global, 360 Degree brand ideas.

The explosion in communications opportunities makes it unrealistic to think we will return to a method of working that encourages the isolation of disciplines. Being able to bring different combinations of media together, or even invent new ones, is a vital (and permanent) feature of the new working habits agencies will have to adopt.

The ultimate goal

Developing working practices cannot be divorced from the corporate ambition. Every 360 Degree agency has, of course, three aims:

- to manage the development of great 360 Degree Brand Ideas that build the client's business
- to grow their own business by winning a greater share of the entire marketing budget
- to cultivate the highest level of interface with the client — and at CEO-level if possible.

None of these can happen if an agency works on a piecemeal, per-project, per-discipline basis, fighting over clients and P&L, stumbling over narrow ideas, and always answering briefs from one, repetitive perspective. Media is infinite. So should the response be.

Responding to complexity

We would all acknowledge that these days marketing is operating in an environment of constant fragmentation and evolution, and, therefore, that complexity is a given. There are no simple solutions any more. Brands, as we have seen, are slippery, amorphous collections of touch-points, some controllable, others not.

360 Degree Branding® is therefore itself a changing and amorphous discipline. There are fewer and fewer "standard responses" to marketing problems. Solutions are becoming "media-bespoke", complex collections of activities that seek to resonate and create interplay amongst themselves.

360 Degree agencies such as Ogilvy & Mather have therefore had to respond in two key ways: to continuously expand the range of specialist disciplines they offer, and to become more and more flexible in how those specialist disciplines combine and collaborate.

Ogilvy & Mather Group, Singapore, is a good micro example of this in action. At last count, the agency group (headcount 250) was capable of identifying 18 distinct specialist marketing disciplines within its walls (see Figure 10.1).

Figure 10.1: The Ogilvy Group, Singapore

1. Advertising
2. Direct Marketing
3. CRM Consultancy
4. Interactive Web Marketing
5. Sales Promotions
6. Public Relations
7. Telemarketing
8. Design
9. Corporate Identity Consultancy
10. Events Management
11. Sponsorship Management
12. Premiums & Branded Merchandise
13. Crisis Management
14. Network Marketing (SMS/E-mail)
15. Guerrilla Marketing
16. Media Training
17. Film & TV Production
18. Strategic Marketing Consultancy

Each has a distinct philosophy and way of working as a single discipline, focusing on a core competence within the 360 Degree framework. Figure 10.2 shows how this works for two of the larger disciplines within the Ogilvy family.

Such diversity — from the TV commercial to logo design, from events management to crisis management — carries several implications:

Figure 10.2 Understanding the Disciplines

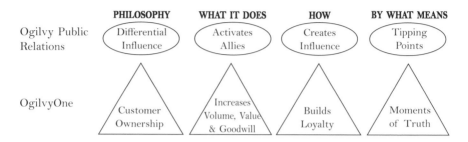

	PHILOSOPHY	WHAT IT DOES	HOW	BY WHAT MEANS
Ogilvy Public Relations	Differential Influence	Activates Allies	Creates Influence	Tipping Points
OgilvyOne	Customer Ownership	Increases Volume, Value & Goodwill	Builds Loyalty	Moments of Truth

1. Brand understanding is shared collateral

No two sets of professionals skilled in different areas can come together to work productively on a project without a common understanding. In the brand communications industry, that is *brand understanding*.

This is the common ground that ALL must share and own. All too often in the past, conventional agencies allowed brand understanding to be the private preserve of one or two key team members — an account director or a planner.

Under a 360 Degree *modus operandi* this simply will not work. Each member of a 360 Degree team must be in possession of a clear and workable understanding of the brand in all its facets: from the business background (what category it operates in, who it competes against, how it is faring), to the brand DNA (the unchangeable essence of the brand), to an intimate knowledge of the consumer (his/her lifestyles, habits and attitudes).

Any and every team member needs to be conversant with all these details. There is no room for a division between "those who know", and "those who don't". 360 Degree Branding® is about collaboration, not delegation.

2. There must be collective responsibility for brand equity

The flip side of empowering all with a clear set of brand understanding is the concept of collective responsibility for the brand and its equity. In every facet of a 360 Degree brand activity that a particular discipline develops, they need to have an acute sense that everything they do will change the consumers' perceptions of a brand. They therefore need to be sure they are altering that perception in a positive and "on-brand" way.

In other words, each discipline needs to understand the difference between "input" and "out-take" — the difference between the activities they implement for the brand and the meaning these create in the mind of the consumer. The two are rarely the same.

Under a 360 Degree model, a brand is a collective responsibility. We are all brand stewards.

3. There is no such thing as a hierarchy of ideas

Ideas are the life-blood of any creative agency. They need to flow freely, constantly and from all directions. A brand needs to be a catalyst for ideas.

However, under the old-fashioned, integration-style model of working, there is a clear hierarchy of ideas. Because it "owns" the bigger budget, the advertising agency often assumes it is at the head of the feeding trough. And at the head of that queue are the advertising creatives. Ideas are allegedly their preserve. Once they've had their precious "big idea", it is passed downstream to other disciplines for them to make what they can of it.

A 360 Degree way of working needs to be more meritocratic. Ideas need to come to the table from all quarters. For starters, the marketing solution to the business problem may not even include advertising! The Promotions and Events specialists may need to own and drive the ideas for the brand. Nowhere are the so-called rules of brainstorming better adhered to than in a flat 360 Degree team of equals who all contribute different perspectives and expertise to bring marketing programs to life.

4. From now on, everyone is both generalist and specialist

Within a 360 Degree brand communications agency, the work processes demand that team members are capable of switching between functioning as brand generalists and as discipline specialists.

A PR director needs to be able to participate in identifying a Brand Challenge and building a Brand Idea; to evaluate ideas from all quarters as to whether or not they meet the singular Challenge facing the brand and contribute to the client's business. Then, they need to be able to switch back to make sure that the PR program influences the right people, the Sales Promotion activates in the right way and that all parts of the program work effectively together.

As a quick reminder, the rules of brainstorming are:

a) Look to generate many ideas
b) Look for wild and different ideas
c) Avoid judgment of ideas — other people's and your own
d) Build on each other's ideas
e) All ideas are recorded.

Getting the right people

Working in this way is a new approach to agency working, one that requires the right type of person to staff it. This is paramount because the only asset agencies have is their people. David Ogilvy's timeless advice to us all is to hire people who are bigger than ourselves. That way, we'll grow, they'll grow and the agency will grow. But the question remains, how to spot those "giants"?

Seven years ago, Miles Young, the Chairman of Ogilvy & Mather in Asia-Pacific, wrote down the key traits and characteristics that lend themselves to the way 360 Degree brand communications is structured and that influence the Agency's selection of people:

Agility: People who are nimble in the way they behave; who are not content to follow the normal path of doing things; who are prepared to cut corners; and who are comfortable at crossing boundaries.

Passion: People who tingle with excitement when they see something that's great; who follow their instincts as to what's good or bad; who have an infectious enthusiasm and the ability to stimulate others with it.

Bravery: People who act quickly and decisively; who are prepared to take risks now and then; who know when to make a stand when it's needed; and who can help others carry the day.

Accountability: People who keep their promises; who see things through to the end; who know where the buck stops; who don't hide from the consequence of what they are doing; and who take pride in achieving goals.

Curiosity: People who have a thirst to know more; who are not content to get by with what they are told; who find out new things for themselves and delight in applying them; who are able to turn knowledge into better insight.

However, even with the right kind of people in place, there must be a corporate mission to avoid losing track of the basics.

Back to basics: Observation

There is no better way to find out new things than by simply observing. The role of the observer in our business has been seriously overlooked. We need to be able to see what is out there in the world affecting our brand. That impartial, objective point of view that only outsiders can give an account team is so often missing.

Agencies tend to only bother undertaking some half-hearted observation when new business comes a-calling. But is it the same for ongoing accounts? Or are we too stuck behind our desks to observe what is really going on? So, let's all get out and about more often, into the streets and where our target customers are. Or at least, let's get beyond the ubiquitous focus group and tracking study, and find out what is *really* influencing the brand and its buyers.

Back to basics: Passion and intuition

What do we mean by this? Perhaps we should cast an eye back to our roots ...

> *"Once you were an artist. Once you were an explorer, a poet, a musician, an actor, and an athlete. Once you were everything you could imagine.*
>
> *Once you were a child. As a two-year-old, you did not have mental patterns or expectations. You had not yet wired your brain to see the world, so everything you encountered was new — presenting you with unlimited learning possibilities. You were unlimited potential and boundless energy seeking direction."*
>
> Stephen Eiffert

The naivety of children is refreshing at times. They make us think, or, rather, *re-think* many of the things we take for granted. Once you become too close to a culture (for example, an organizational or a brand culture), it is too easy just to do things by remote control. Nothing is new any more, nothing startling, nothing out of the ordinary.

We carry on with our annual plans, doggedly determined to squeeze another share point out of our deadly competitors; always doing the same things, because we have not opened our eyes to the opportunity to do things differently.

But, take another look! It is this "adult" behavior that is *extraordinary*. As the actress Rita Mae Brown once opined: "Insanity is doing the same thing over and over again, expecting something different to happen."

Back to basics: Selling ideas

Every agency needs passion and intuition in everything it does. And this type of energy needs to be taken all the way through to the "selling" of ideas to clients.

We have to remember that selling ideas is about taking someone on an emotional journey as much as (and perhaps more than) providing them with a logical reason "why". So, people need to transform the "selling" process into a "stimulation" process; to *stimulate* clients, and not evaluate each execution one by one in great detail.

Rather, they should be stimulated to explore the full and forward potential of the Idea, the opportunities for expanding on the Idea, and the chance to make that Idea one of the very cornerstones of their business.

The practicalities of working the "new way"

- **Who is on the team?**
  When establishing the working practices of a 360 Degree Branding® agency, the brand team leader's role is vital. He or she will need to choose team members very carefully to guarantee cross-discipline diversity, ownership and commitment from those doing the work, and the involvement of the client. It is important, too, to ensure that the team has the right number of people to prevent it from becoming counter-productive.

- **When to meet?**
  The best practice we have developed at Ogilvy is when many of these working practices are a daily normal reality. We suggest a brand team meet en masse at least four times during the course of creating and implementing a 360 Degree Branding® solution. These meetings would be for:

  Analysis: to focus on the issues facing the brand, to interrogate its infrastructure and to develop the key brand challenge

  Development: to develop and brainstorm ideas that meet the brand challenge

Arrangement: to bring together all implementation plans for cohesion with a target consumer analysis — the purpose being to maximize the number and quality of the points of contact

Evaluation: to find out what works and what doesn't; what creates interplay and what doesn't; what meets the brand challenge and what doesn't; what is right for the brand and what isn't.

- **Who leads the charge?**
  Collaboration does not necessarily mean "democracy". For a 360 Degree team to function, there needs to be just one arbiter of brand ideas, one back-stop who can call a halt to idea-production, and can oversee idea-implementation.

  In a perfect world, there is a brand team leader who serves as a catalyst. Ideally, this person is skilled at bringing together the group to generate new thinking; is skilled at client relations and understands the client's business; and can recognize a big brand idea when he or she hears one.

  But also let's not forget that an agency is in business too. The best team leaders understand enough about the various P&Ls in play (theirs and their client's) to push for opportunities that maximize the agency's capabilities and revenue.

- **Who facilitates?**
  In Ogilvy & Mather Asia-Pacific, the Account Planner has been thrust into the midst of the 360 Degree process. No one better exemplifies the way in which this new way of working requires range and flexibility than the Planner.

  Traditionally, the Planner has been the "voice of the consumer" within the agency — the sole repository of knowledge about the brand–consumer relationship. In this role, the Planner has been freed from the tyranny of opinionated Creative Directors and clients, and is able to look dispassionately at the proposed activity, measure it against a bank of consumer knowledge and know whether it is right for the brand, and good for business.

Within a 360 Degree operation, the Planner has to be able to work comfortably with each and every discipline, to be equally at home with Public Relations campaigns and Direct Marketing mailshots. In other words, the Planner has to know how each of the various discipline executions can or should involve the consumer or influence a third party. The new-generation planner is required to work horizontally in a traditionally vertical world.

Facilitation is one of their primary skill requirements. Managing and getting the best out of the diverse team members is the critical new core competence.

- **What products and tools to use?**
  Agencies are the same the world over in certain respects — they all love to have tools they can show clients and new employees. Most of these tools can be very valuable and can greatly assist in the smooth functioning of working practices.

  Ogilvy & Mather is no different. We have a number of tools to assist in the development of 360 Degree brand communications. But, remember that clients aren't interested in tools or processes. They are interested in the solutions we provide. We should avoid the temptation to show off our tools to our clients.

- **Who has the ideas?**
  As we said earlier, ideas are the lifeblood of a flat, meritocratic 360 Degree agency. But this creates a curious obligation — ideas become the responsibility of everyone.

  Most agencies and clients would find it hard to conceive of a creative department outside the advertising or one-to-one departments. And yet, at a round-table brand team ideas session, sometimes these "creatives" can be blinkered about anything other than advertising or one-to-one ideas. It is not their fault. As with haute cuisine, if you rely only on the sous-chef who specializes in sauces, your meal will lack substance.

Now, the floor is open for Sales Promotion to put its own creative (ideas) teams together, for Sponsorship to contribute on the same level playing field as the Cannes-awarded creative director. Bringing together a keen brand understanding and the expertise of a particular field of marketing creates an obligation on all to be "creatives".

- **Who manages the client?**

Similarly, the canvas for account management — getting and delivering the best for your client and his/her brand — is broadened to take in a much wider range than the traditional point-man. We all now work in account management.

Providing 360 Degree solutions means being truly "media-neutral". Recommendations can only be truly neutral if there are no vested interests at play to swing things. Everyone is under pressure to deliver numbers, to make stretch targets, to fill the new business gap. The pressure is such that it could, of course, influence the decision about which way a media selection will go. Go to an advertising executive and you get a 30-second TV solution. Go to a Public Relations executive and you get a press release. Same problem, same strategy, different solution.

Such behavior is not in the interests of managing a client's marketing budget in a responsible and effective way. It has no place in a 360 Degree brand communications agency.

The answer is simple. It would be better for P&Ls to be organized around brands, not disciplines. This is a simple (but radical) change of financial culture, and a new way of thinking, which can allow media neutrality to thrive.

The bigger picture of collaboration

What does everyone do? How does it all fit together?

To answer these questions, here is a brief description of seven of the major disciplines and their respective roles in 360 Degree brand communications.

Advertising

Of course, the ultimate objective of advertising is to sell more "stuff". This is the absolute reason why advertising agencies exist. As David Ogilvy said about his agency, "we sell or else". However, these days, most advertising agencies share a clear vision of the best way to achieve sales — through an emphasis on "the brand".

By understanding the relationship between the consumer and the brand, agencies seek to build and then leverage the power of the brand.

When it comes to the output itself, advertising's major roles are twofold: to create awareness and interest in a brand and to build values and personality for that brand.

However, this is also the general purpose of many other disciplines. At Ogilvy & Mather, it is recognized that advertising alone is rarely sufficient to achieve marketing objectives because the points at which a consumer comes into contact with a brand or its communications are increasingly varied. O&M Advertising views advertising as only one of several marketing communications disciplines, all of which are integrated around a Brand Idea.

However, advertising is often the brand's only unfair advantage. So, whichever agency is responsible for producing it, it had better make an impact and it had better be relevant.

Questions for your advertising agency:

- Do you have a good understanding of the brand's equity?
- Do you have a full and rich picture of the world of the

brand's customers, and how do they connect with the brand in their world?

- Do you have a clear understanding of what social changes are taking place that will influence the brand?
- What is the "Brand Idea"?
- Do the brand's communications truly differentiate it from the competition, even if there are no discernible product differences?

One-to-one Marketing and CRM

This discipline seeks to leverage brand equity disproportionately with the key 20% of customers who account for, on average, 80% of sales. Developing a brand relationship with these high-value customers and nurturing that relationship is the prime objective.

This will first involve "capturing" customers who fit this preferred profile, usually by gathering data and screening it. This therefore requires the capability for data management.

Second, it involves striking up a one-to-one dialogue with that customer. Obviously, for that to work, the content of that dialogue must be highly tailored to that customer — in other words, data profiling is paramount. The aim of this is to build emotional loyalty for the brand, thus driving customer retention.

Third, the process will often involve cross-selling or up-selling. Given the quality of the relationship between the customer and the brand, this is easier to achieve. However, too much selling can sour a customer's attitude to the CRM (customer relationship management) program.

The tools of the CRM trade involve clear and robust analysis of customer segmentation and clustering, database management, intricate contact-strategy management, a clear understanding of brand equity, creative solutions and telemarketing.

Questions for your CRM agency:

- Do you know how the brand customers segment in terms of high-volume sectors, compared to its competitors?
- Where is the biggest movement in the customer base — in acquisition, retention or growth?
- Can you communicate with each individual customer by name?
- Is the customer payback known at a cluster or an individual level?
- How do high-value customers differ in their behavior and purchasing patterns?
- Is customer loyalty driven by financial, behavioral or emotional factors? How is this being measured?

Interactive Marketing

This discipline combines brand building with technical interactive skills to enable brands to use the latest media to most effect. Interactive marketing ought to be about building brand experiences, whether building brand image, communicating brand messages, or developing one-to-one relationships.

It needs to be highly strategic, business orientated and centered on a clear appreciation of brand equity. It should also encompass a wide range of interactive technologies, from web to desktop to mobile phones. It can also be a highly effective discipline for providing detailed information, ongoing dialogue and sales promotional support. Only for certain categories, and where security features are seen to be adequate by consumers, is it a good medium for the end-sale.

Questions for your Interactive agency:

- What role does interactive play as a part of the overall communication strategy?

- What benefits does it offer that will encourage consumers to want an ongoing relationship and return usage?
- What information is gathered about users, and how is it used for marketing purposes?
- What volume of traffic do you generate via interactive communications? How is this benchmarked?
- How well are interactive programs integrated into the broader brand strategy?

Sales Promotions and Events

This discipline spans the breadth of expertise from strategic to tactical; from creating promotional concepts that fit with core brand equity, to designing, sourcing and fulfilling promotional mechanics and, finally, evaluation.

This discipline is focused on activating sales, mainly at the point of purchase, but in a way that also builds (or at least does not undermine) brand values.

Activation can include extensive field operations, door-to-door selling, sampling, in-store promotions, on-pack promotions, outdoor events, merchandising, production of point-of-sale materials, exhibitions and distribution analysis.

Questions for your Promotions agency:

- Are current promotions planned to meet specific long-term objectives, or do they tend to be short-term and tactical only?
- Are there detailed promotional plans for each brand?
- How effective are the promotions you run? Does all activity get evaluated? How?
- What is the value of genuine new sales generated by the promotion (as distinct from simply subsidizing existing customers, or bringing forward purchases they would have made at a later date)?

Public Relations

Public relations help influence the people who influence the reputation of brands. It is focused on strengthening corporate reputations, helping organizations to grow and change, raising capital, enlisting allies, aligning employees behind the corporate vision, working with governments, handling crises and managing issues.

The skill-sets that a PR company can draw upon are extensive: research, strategy formulation, counseling, CEO support, shareholder communications, product-launch, publicity media and investor relations, awareness and education campaigns, government access, event management, and communications and media training.

Questions for your PR agency:

- How much favorable attention (e.g. media coverage) does the brand receive?
- How do professional experts feel about recommending the brand? Whose endorsement would help?
- Are there any issues which the brand could own, or potential issues it needs to avert?
- Does the brand publicly live up to its promises?
- Is the brand a good citizen of its community?
- How do the brand's employees feel about being associated with it? Is their behavior in line with the brand's values?

Brand Identity

Brand Identity "consultants" advise corporations on their brand and identity strategy to help them achieve a unique profile. This reaches a critical point at a time of mergers and acquisitions, or when the corporate identity is clearly out of step with the evolving marketplace.

Their approach is to blend the complementary skills of strategic analysis, creative thinking, design and organizational implementation. They provide advice on market positioning, brand architecture, proposition development and the operational implications of a chosen brand promise, while creative teams bring imaginative expression to the brand. This is then brought to life within the client's business by internal communications programs and workshops.

Any corporation will be concerned with the way that those exposed to that business think and feel about it. There are therefore many audiences which need consideration when creating a corporate brand strategy — some are discrete but, increasingly, many overlap: customers, employees, stakeholders, business partners, opinion-formers ... even those who have no intention of buying that company's products or services.

Questions for your Brand Identity agency:

- Are customers clear on what the brand stands for? Does the brand have a clear identity for them?
- How well do all the design elements support the overall proposition?
- What is the strategy to create alignment among all the stakeholders?
- Is the brand being used to build a lasting, mutually rewarding relationship with its stakeholders?

Immersion Marketing

With many of the above disciplines, a brand is dependent on *passive* absorption of its messages. But, it is easy for consumers to ignore commercial messages, and many do. To overcome this avoidance, we need immersion techniques, to *actively* absorb consumers *in* the action, rather than parade the message in front of them. At least, that is the mandate of Immersion Marketing.

Immersive marketing programs are a unique mixture of planned and unplanned activity, strategic brand thinking and media insight. They utilize new and ambient media, but also new combinations of old media to stage brand events that ensnare a customer in a series of orchestrated brand "hits". Immersion promotions feed off guerrilla and viral techniques, as well as traditional above-the-line activities.

Guerrilla Marketing: This involves marketing that is unconventional, non-traditional, not by-the-book, and extremely flexible. It is designed to achieve conventional goals, such as building awareness, by using unconventional methods that "ambush" the consumer.

Viral Marketing: Whatever you call it this week — propagation marketing, inertia marketing, or even contagion marketing — viral marketing is a simple but powerful way to get noticed by an ever-increasing audience.

Simply put, viral marketing is advertising that spreads itself as viruses do — the tagline at the bottom of every message you send from your free e-mail account, the holiday screen-saver you received from everyone you know. You get it, you pass it on — that's viral. Viral techniques work because people will always pass messages along to others. As many as 81% of those receiving viral marketing pass it on to at least one other person, and almost half will pass the viral message to two or three people.

Questions for your Immersion Marketing agency:

- How sophisticated is your consumer at avoiding marketing messages?
- Who are the key influencers? What are the new media opportunities to get to them?
- What sort of experience does your brand need to underwrite?

- Do you need to change the way you sell?
- How brave are you prepared to be?

There are, of course, no simple solutions; just a lot of hard work, and a shared ambition. As the old proverb goes: "None of us is as strong as all of us." If the will is not there throughout the organisation, the task will be mighty hard. The following case study on American Express shows how effective the process can be when the different experts work cohesively together.

CASE STUDY 8

American Express "Blue" (Singapore) — A new card for a new generation

Background

American Express is a very well-known global brand — one that has endured in a fiercely competitive market because it has had such a strong presence. People know what the brand is, that it stands for accountability, personal success and achievement. It's a badge of honor. It signifies "You've arrived". That sense of arrival may be expressed in different ways in different cultures, but everywhere the brand has one clear identity.

But this very identity — while such an asset with its core target — was off-putting to the growing younger consumers who saw the card as an "old, rich guy's brand".

Moreover, in some markets, the pay-as-you-go charge-card structure, which is at the heart of the brand's accountability attribute, was a competitive disadvantage where revolving credit has more appeal.

The challenge was how to extend the American Express brand franchise to include a credit card that would appeal to this younger, more credit-conscious group.

To do that, American Express needed to invent a card that had all the essence of American Express, yet would be seen as different, younger, hipper, cooler, more modern. Thus, the American Express Blue Card was born.

Understanding who and why

The key to understanding the Blue Card is to understand the consumers it was designed for. While credit cards are a fact of everyday life — a necessity, almost a commodity — their owners are not.

There was a huge market of consumers who saw their financial transactions in a different and distinctive way, and wanted products and services that reflected that. These consumers shared less a demographic than a mindset. To them, success meant more than mere wealth; it meant being in control of one's life.

These consumers are independent, proactive and entrepreneurial in spirit. What we found in our research was that this segment was not really being tapped into in any significant way by the traditional credit cards. So this was American Express's opportunity.

Singapore Blues

The Blue Card was first introduced in Singapore in 1998. What started out as a conventional direct-mail template brief turned into a much larger and involving program.

Amex offers rates carrot with new credit card

By **Clarissa Tan**

[SINGAPORE] American Express yesterday rocked Singapore's already saturated credit card market with the launch of its own credit card — at promotional interest rates that are up to half the 24 per cent Visa and Master charge for rollover credit.

After issuing charge cards for years, Amex recently launched its new blue Amex credit card in the region.

At yesterday's launch for Singapore, Amex country manager Anthony Lee said unpaid balances on the new card will carry an interest of 15.9 per cent per year.

This preferential rate is valid only for the first six months of an account provided the cardholder applies for the card by Dec 31.

And to win over existing Visa and Master cardmem-

bers, Amex is offering them an annual interest of only 11.9 per cent for the first six months of membership for any rollover balances transferred to its new card. This is less than half the 24 per cent per annum charged by Visa and MasterCard issuing banks, and is also lower than the rate slapped on many clean overdraft accounts.

Issuing banks for Master-

Card and Visa yesterday said they were unfazed by Amex's aggressive offer. Visa's senior country manager Richard Chang said that while there would be an impact on the card market, the impact would be "anything but significant" for Visa. "The member banks (who issue Visa) are very, very used to competition," he said.

Continued on Pg 2

On guard: *Amex is going on an interest rates offensive with its new blue card launched yesterday*

ARTHUR LEE

Initial press coverage preparing the ground for launch

The way "Blue" was packaged was key, offering the audience a way to survive the economic downturn that Singapore was experiencing at the time. The package offered the lowest interest rate in town, no annual joining fee and balance transfer, whilst carrying with it the positive attributes of the mother brand. In short, this meant being in tune with the audience — behaving wisely, shopping freely.

The American Express Card has always been a classic. As the BrandPrint reads: "It is not for everybody. It is for those who think bigger thoughts, do bigger things and paint bigger pictures." "Blue" was to be the modern version of that classic, updated and relevant, with product attributes that reflected the modern consumer.

"Blue moves with you. Blue stands for the excitement you feel about the emerging opportunities in your world: a young, fun, aggressive, energetic attitude that says "Blue is new and enhances the life you lead". It's fresh, modern, hip, active, optimistic and always forward-thinking."

The Brand Idea

And so was born the Brand Idea. "It's cool to be Blue" appealed to the heart but also positioned Blue at the rational level as the card that gives you better control (the accountability trait that exists in the original brand).

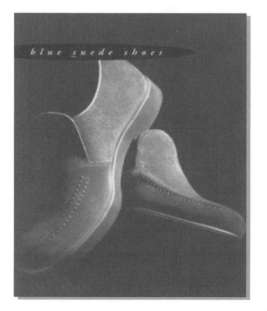

Pre-launch press teaser ensuring "It's cool to be Blue"

Working together

360 Degree brand involvement requires several messages to multiple contacts across many different media channels. This in turn requires multi-discipline collaboration, a new development for an industry that has traditionally specialized in building discipline-specific business units that resemble (and behave like) silos.

In the traditional allocation of marketing resources, one communication was predominantly used to answer each equity of the brand: advertising to address image; public relations to address goodwill; relationship marketing to address customer segments; promotions to address channels; and so on.

In that traditional process, TV advertising was often the driving force for other communication. It was where the most money was spent. However, in today's altered brand landscape, every communication can (and often must) have an impact on each equity of the brand.

It is vital therefore that a collaborative, coordinated approach is managed between and across disciplines.

The farming analogy

It was public relations, not television advertising, that led the way in Singapore. PR was the driving force to establish the issue of high interest rates, alerting the target to an issue that our brand was about to solve. To return to the language of our farming analogy, this helped prepare the ground.

PR was then first to provide the solution to this issue — the low Amex Blue interest rate — and a wave of television advertising then helped cut through public inertia. This helped to sow the seeds.

At this point, a coordinated media plan swept across Singapore, ushering in Blue in a big way:

- The web, a favorite medium of this younger audience, contrasted Blue very favorably with the competition, which had never been seen online at all.
- Subway tickets, with the Blue Card printed on the reverse, added a new dimension, highlighting the message of the lowest interest rate in town. This was a new medium and had never before been used by American Express anywhere in the world.
- "Take one" brochures intercepted the young audience at high-traffic points such as Orchard Road, a favorite shopping and eating haunt for Singapore youth.

- Solicitation mailing was cost-effectively targeted at pre-identified audiences.
- Telemarketing, often a peripheral activity in communication, had significant impact on lead generation and conversion, generating up to 23% of sales. Telemarketers were trained in Blue values, with prepared texts allowing even freelance staff (the lifeblood of any telemarketing operation) to understand Blue and inform prospective customers of the benefits it offered.

To continue with our farming analogy, the plants were growing.

But once the card was out there, card members had to be encouraged to use the product time and again, and to feel proud to be a Blue Card member. This presented a key role for relationship marketing and public relations in both protecting the harvest and improving the yield, as any good farmer would do.

Poster in Orchard Road — where the "Blue" consumers hang out

A media plan for collaboration

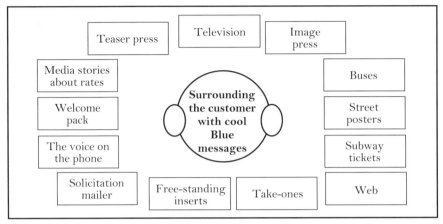

Blue never started, nor indeed continued, with massive television or print advertising. But an interrogation of the product, and its potential younger affluent consumers, helped create a much larger idea and a significantly expanded program, not only for Singapore, but for the world. The program took card communication out of its traditional narrow rut and helped make Blue a sensible response to the environment.

The results

The original acquisition target in Singapore was achieved within 12 weeks of launch. The original target was revised upwards by 50% and was met before the end of December 1998.

Building on the Singapore approach, the launch of American Express Blue in the United States shattered the aggressive acquisition goals by 141%. As Harvey Golub, Chairman and CEO of American Express, remarked, "It was a grand slam. The most successful product launch in American Express history."

Shelly Lazarus, Chairman of Ogilvy & Mather Worldwide, commented: "What added immeasurably to the launch was the nature of the collaboration: different disciplines responsible for different pieces of the client's business units, working together to create a communication launch for a technologically advanced product, spanning almost every conceivable medium."

Here, indeed, was collaboration in action.

BEIJING BICYCLES

There are now about 1,500 million bicycles in the world, of which 470 million (almost one-third) reside in China. For every 100 families living in China's cities, there are 160 bikes (but "only" 80 bikes per 100 families in rural areas). No wonder China is unanimously acknowledged as the kingdom of bicycles.

The capital of this kingdom is Beijing, where there are estimated to be 11 million bikes, making it one of the cities with the densest bike population in the world. Why so many?

Beijing is very flat, and many big factories and research institutes are located on the outskirts of the city; so large numbers of people have to commute. The simplest way is by bike. Downtown, the layout of the inner city resembles a chessboard, and the alleys or narrow streets are more convenient for bikes than for buses or trolley buses. Here, amongst the *hutongs*, the bicycle is not only a way to get around, but a business vehicle, even a status symbol. There are broom vendors, knife sharpeners, coal-briquette sellers, all on bicycles winding around the back lanes trying to make a living.

With so many bikes, it was only a matter of time before they became used for advertising. Currently, advertisers have two options — "solid wheel" advertising, or "the *peleton*".

Solid-wheel bike advertising is an idea imported from Europe, where wheels and frame are painted to create maximum impact. Still in its infancy as a medium, it looks set to take off around the 2008 Olympics.

The other option for advertisers, "the *peleton*", consists of 15 riders, suited-up in neon-yellow jackets and matching baseball caps, riding 15 identical bikes *in formation* around the busiest of Beijing's streets. Looking remarkably like refugees from the Tour de France, they have proved to be an arresting sight. Retailer Ai Jia World Furniture is behind the ads, and they have about 100 riders out at any given time. The men in the bright yellow jackets have become part of the gray urban landscape, snaking along the roadside like a giant neon caterpillar. At bus stops, team leaders sometimes order the team to alight and mingle with the passengers, silently cultivating Ai Jia brand recognition.

"There are many furniture stores in Beijing now and we had to do something to distinguish ourselves," said Chen Cuili, the company's stylish young advertising director. "It's been very effective. It's new and it's interesting. A lot of customers say they've noticed." The year-old company is one of many huge furniture stores that have sprung up recently to cater to China's new house-proud urban middle class who, for the first time, can own their own homes and have the money to decorate them. And the Chinese Ai Jia (which means "love home") must, of course, distinguish itself from the powerful new import, Yi Jia ("pleasant home"), known in the West as IKEA.

Chen's main concern is the campaign's effectiveness compared to TV advertising. "It's hard to compare costs," she said. "There are so many people watching TV, but they may not notice you because there are so many ads." The fact that it is feasible to use teams of humans as moving billboards says a lot about the strange inconsistencies in China's economy, where ordinary workers' wages have often not changed that much from Communist-era rates, but prices of goods and commodities — including advertising — are more in line with Western capitalism. People are cheap, whereas billboards and television ads are fantastically expensive.

While obviously a growing media opportunity, bicycles are also a wonderful source of cultural insight into China too, so intrinsic are they to life there. For example, it is said that Beijing's latest traffic war between bikes and cars is a perfect illustration of the proverb "the soft and gentle will defeat the hard and obstinate" (*yi rou ke gang*). Bicycles have ruled the road since Liberation in China and they are certainly not about to give up without a fight. Or, indeed, for an interesting political insight, consider the curiously similar language of U.S. President Herbert Hoover who, in a speech in 1928, promised his people "a chicken in every pot", and Deng Xiaoping's famous campaign promise from the 1970s: "A Flying Pigeon in every household" (Flying Pigeon being the most famous brand of bicycle in China). And the bicycle is also inspiring art too: *Beijing Bicycles*, a remake of the 1940s Italian classic film *The Bicycle Thief*, is winning international acclaim for young Chinese film-maker Wang Xiaoshuai.

Synchronized bicycling — a new Olympic sport?

Conclusion

The Pacific Century —
the Future of Brands in Asia

"Young people, go East."
John Naisbitt, *MegaTrends Asia*

Some historians have declared that the 19th century was "the European Century", that the 20th century belonged to America, and that the 21st Century will be "the Pacific Century" — when the Asian nations will emerge as the political, economic and cultural powerhouse of the world. Some 65% of the world's wealth is already located on the Pacific Rim, and 65% of the world's population currently reside there. Asian and Pacific communities already are vital to the health of the international economy.

However, the diverse societies of this vast and vibrant region are still undergoing phenomenal change as they adapt to an interconnected world influenced by the rapid development of technology and communication. In the midst of these changes, the tremendous macro-forces that shape and influence the consumer markets of Asia are creating opportunities and threats for brands and their marketers.

In this concluding chapter, we want to ask the question "who is best positioned to take advantage of the opportunities that the Pacific Century will provide?" To answer that, we need to re-open (and re-define) the long debate about multinational vs local brands — who (if either) has the upper hand?

The shape of things to come?

Looking into the future (always a hazardous exercise!), let us highlight three things that are likely to radically alter the *brandscape* in Asia's biggest markets as the century progresses.

We highlight these three "predictions" because they sharpen our focus onto one very important dynamic in particular — the ongoing struggle between multinational (read *Western*) brands, and locally owned or based *Asian* brands.

China — fast learners in Branding

China's entry into the World Trade Organization (WTO) has been called the single most important economic event for Asia since economic reforms began in China more than two decades ago. In the same way as Britain dominated the Industrial Revolution in the 19th century, so it is generally accepted that China is set to become the workhorse of the world in the next decades.

WTO accession opens China up to an influx of foreign brands. Since 1978 and until recently, the expansion of the market has been dominated by big name Western brands (often referred to as *"ming pai"*). The hidden assumption has been that local Chinese brands (or *"pai zi"*) would fall by the wayside under the onslaught of sophisticated Western marketing techniques.

But, the Chinese government has long been aware of the importance of building strong local brands to compete on equal footing once the trade barriers come down. As state-owned enterprises have moved into the private sector, expertise in branding has been actively encouraged by the central government. And, there have been some notable success stories for local brands over the years: Olive shampoo, Haier electronics, Legend computers, and many others.

However, the difficulty these and other local favorites face is the big issue of identifying and owning enduring brand values that can sustain market share positions. In our analysis of the complete WPP BrandZ database, we found that the Chinese consumer *claims* to be more "price-sensitive" and less "brand loyal" than consumers in other markets, but actually prove to have a *higher* loyalty.

The problem is that this "loyalty" tends to be a financial loyalty, rather than an emotional loyalty. And, it is the emotional loyalty that builds long-term sales and profit for brands. Take Legend computers. On some measures it has a larger loyal customer base than IBM. Operationally, it has avoided the temptation of introducing old technology; and has supported the first-time user with free software, home-installation and Chinese-oriented software. However, on the key measure of future brand strength (and marketplace performance) — the "Voltage" rating — it comes a poor second to IBM. The reason is that it scores best with older consumers, and least well with Internet users. And e-commerce is where the market is going!

The picture is similar for other categories, whether beer, mobile phones or skincare. Western brands have a stronger "Voltage" than their lower-priced local competitors.

The big question the multinationals face is whether they can fully assimilate the cultural context. Chinese culture is arguably the most symbolic in the world. Yet visual or image literacy is an area that Western marketers rarely explore in depth, believing in the myth that the Chinese consumer is unsophisticated and literal-minded. In our extensive qualitative research over the years, we have found that Chinese consumers respond extremely positively to the kind of culturally sensitive image-based advertising that some foreign brands like Siemens, Motorola, Ericsson and Coca-Cola provide, but many others ignore as they lapse into one stereotype or another.

In short, we find that tried and tested Western-style brand marketing principles work; but that both local and Western brands need to do much more in China to exploit them fully.

India — quick step to quality and customer service

Albert Einstein observed that only "two general truths emerge from the study of history. One is that things change much more, and much more quickly than one might think. The other is that things change much less, and more slowly than one might think." This perspective of history matches the current evolution in branding in India.

India grew up with foreign brands as part of the landscape. Hindustan Lever began operations in 1894, Colgate from the 1920s, Cadbury and Nestlé in the early years following the Second World War. Coca-Cola and IBM were also early entrants, but left after 1976 when the government forced foreign companies to reduce their equity share to under 50%, only to return over the past decade or so as the market has opened up to foreign direct investment.

The issue is not about brand values — these are well established for long-term brand-builders, whether local or multinational. The issues facing branding companies are more structural and service-related.

And here there are paradoxes at play: in such a large, rural and tradition-bound country, long-established companies have the distribution infrastructure in place to expand their product offering, but struggle with lifetime labor laws to create the efficiencies needed to exploit them profitably.

The opposite is the case for newer players. Trade barriers are coming down, albeit too slowly in the eyes of multinationals (who maintain India is still a very difficult market to enter). But even as these barriers are being lifted, allowing them to expand out of their niche market positions, they face real supply-chain management issues in sourcing, productivity and recruitment to avoid the longer-term stored up problems of the established brands.

These can be solved without sacrificing quality, as Tata has shown. A longstanding local truck maker, it moved into the passenger car market in the mid 1990s with the Tata Indica. At first, about two-thirds of its raw materials were imported (with the huge tariffs that go with importing). But, it now claims that 90% of its raw materials and 100% of the steel used are locally sourced. Quality is guaranteed, and the huge economies from local sourcing have helped deliver a big success.

Success stories in manufacturing like this are a rarity. For a developing country, India has an astonishingly high 55% of GDP taken up by the service sector. A more vibrant manufacturing sector may well be needed to create employment. However, the fact is that there is a boom in healthcare and health management, financial services, insurance, software services, consultancies etc.

This service sector boom is also enabling smart Indian companies to consolidate their brand positions. From Titan watches to Cavin Care toiletries and cosmetics to Maruti cars, there are many examples of high-quality customer service programs, proactive call centers and database management relationship marketing programs.

It will not be easy for newer multinational brands to break through against these well-established Indian competitors. One factor in their favor is the collapse in the real estate market over the past few years. Chain stores and shopping malls are now slowly emerging to compete with over seven million "mom & pop" stores across the country. Pizza Hut, McDonald's and KFC are already present in the city centers, and, as a final symbol of globalism perhaps, Starbucks is on its way.

Local Indian brands are going to need to continue the quality and service improvement to cope with the multinational competition when it finally manages to steer its way through to an even playing field.

But, with local competitors already making huge strides in quality and service delivery, multinationals can expect a tough fight, even if the playing field is fully leveled.

Japan — the struggle continues

For a country that burst onto the global branding scene in the 70s and 80s, we see little hope without significant reform to aid a new surge of local brands. The small and medium business sector has historically been the engine of growth and change, as it avoids the stagnating practices of the bigger companies. This is where entrepreneurial flair happens. This is how Honda, Canon, Sony, and Toyota started. To succeed, the SMBs need funding. But, they are being choked of funds, as the banking sector is under severe strain.

Japan, while struggling with deflation and recession, is still the world's largest consumer economy. At the same time, Japanese brands are beginning to take the other Asian markets seriously, especially China (both as a manufacturing base and export market), as its domestic market shrinks under the weight of a rapidly aging population.

Historically, the dominant players have adopted a kind of "build it and they will come" approach to brand-building. Sales is still the dominant business discipline, and trade incentives the prime marketing tool, for many companies. The wholesaler network is intricate, costly to manage, and it drives profits (and hence investment capital) down.

However, we can expect a simpler system to emerge over time. Exceptions are already emerging. Sony is innovating with direct selling over the internet for PCs, offering the Vaio with personalized features instead of a discount. Margins are higher, and Sony by-passes wholesalers. Likewise, Uniqlo, a low-price casual outfitter, produces its clothes in China through a trading company and disregards the wholesaler network.

Another area where companies found themselves boxed in by an ever-more demanding environment for the newest and latest is in technology. Multinational branding companies historically found it very hard to compete with "just in time" production and an obsession with constant innovation. In addition, any technology gap was often compounded by their own inflexibility to meet Japanese cultural needs. Part of the post-war U.S. cultural invasion, Coca-Cola finally found success when it focused on coffee, water and tea rather than its eponymous brand. Procter & Gamble found success with Pampers only when it improved the quality and texture of its diapers to meet local needs.

Where multinationals win is where they relentlessly pursue the strong product brand-building models which have been successful elsewhere. Japanese brands may often have technological leadership, but they have simply not attempted to brand themselves in a way that gives consumers an understanding of what the brand really stands for.

This is both an Achilles heel and odd, given that, culturally, Japan is extending its influence across Asia. Japan may be in no mood to invest in the region (its banking system is under severe strain), but from television drama to pop music to comics to sophisticated animated games to food to the purity of "zen" living to cute toys, Japan's influence is wide-ranging. In all these areas, Japan instinctively knows the power and role of branding, and in a very 360 Degree way.

Yet, in its home market entrenched practices make true brand-building a rarity. Agencies are focused on selling media, not building brands, their business model elevating "brand awareness" to the all-important factor. But this does not guarantee protection from well-branded competitors. Kao, despite vastly superior awareness, trial rates, distribution and sales support, has been washed away by Lever's Dove in both the personal wash and shampoo categories. Starbucks, only operating in urban centers and despite a no-smoking policy in one of the world's heaviest smoking countries, has surged past imitators who claimed first-mover advantage.

Additionally, there is a big question hanging over Japanese business: how the market will adapt to the massive changes in demography. Will local brands adjust to the most rapidly aging population in the world? Only 5% of brand marketing budgets are currently targeted at the over 50s — but almost a third, rising to over 40% over the next few years, of the population are part of this "golden generation". They are different from their elders: they grew up during the post World War Two era of U.S. cultural infusion. They do not have an allergy to foreign things, or foreign brands.

And, if the entrenched local brands are not really brands, then unless they change quickly, further misery will likely be in store for Japanese business.

The future

These three developments all fan the flames of the established and ongoing debate in the "brand community" about which brands are best placed to capitalize on these market changes. So, to whom does the future belong?

Great Asian brands

Can you name 10 global (non-Japanese) Asian brands? Can you name 10 strong regional Asian brands?

Not easy, is it? Once prompted, you may well know many more than 10 of each, of course; but the point is that they don't spring easily to mind. We suspect that in 10 years, this task will be a no-brainer. Both Singapore and China have stated a desire to create up to 10 world class brands in 10 different industries within the next 10 years. A tall order, but by no means impossible in today's accelerated consumer culture. China perhaps will look to leverage its existing expertise in areas such as the bicycle and the air-conditioning sectors. Singapore could look to newer industries (such as "life sciences" and biotechnology) to supply the brands, as well as creative services industries that probably don't currently exist.

So much for the future. Today great Asian brands appear to

be few and far between. At a cursory glance, it would seem that
Asian brands are a long way behind their multinational
counterparts — indeed, it is often said there are only a few truly
powerful Asian brands, and that Asian businesses spend too
much time considering short-term gains and operational
efficiencies to worry about long-term issues like branding.
However, this view is a long way short of the truth, and a closer
inspection shows why.

Asian brands moving ahead?

It is true that in 1997–98, the larger multinationals seemed to be
having it their own way. When the first Asian crisis hit, it was
these deep-pocketed multinationals that mopped up cheap
market share, and even cheaper local players. The local brands,
many with U.S. dollar loans, were crucified by fluctuating
exchange rates and devalued currencies. Unable to fight back,
many lacking both the financial resources and the marketing
savvy to compete, local brands suffered across the board.

But more recently, the pendulum seems to be swinging back
the other way — local brands are staging a remarkable come-
back. Take China, for example. In 2000, 12 of the top 14
advertisers were local manufacturers and, in 2001, the entire top
10 biggest-spending brands were local brands (*Source:* AC
Nielsen). Leading international brand Coca-Cola ranked only
20th among the most advertised products.

Despite the greater marketing sophistication of the
multinationals, China's local brands were doing extremely well.
In a recent Gallup poll, seven out of the top 10 most-recognized
brands were Chinese — with Wahaha, Bank of China and
Changhong (TV sets) relegating even the mighty Coca-Cola to a
mere fourth. The same survey also showed that Chinese
consumers were exhibiting a marked preference for local brands
— 80% of respondents preferring to buy Chinese-branded
goods, and a similar number (79%) claiming preference for

products that are made in China. This could not be dismissed as mere patriotic sentiment — by far the majority of consumers asked (69%) felt that the "Made in China" stamp was a positive endorsement of product quality.

To all of this, add the fact that the price of local brands is generally lower, and they seem to hold the enviable position of being able to offer both perceived quality *and* perceived value.

Investing in brand equity

Many Asian companies have realized the power of the brand, and have invested accordingly. Part of this has been a reaction to the 1997 crisis. Large numbers of Asian companies realized that those who operate in several global markets are less vulnerable than those who operate solely in their country of origin. And a strong brand helps companies compete internationally, as well as enabling them to defend their share at home from the ever-present demand for foreign brands. One of the most-cited examples of this is Haier, the Chinese appliance manufacturer, which now has a factory in the U.S. and 25% market share of the U.S. small refrigerator market.

Asian brands league table

This "awakening of the brand" in Asia has also led to the phenomenon of league tables on the top brands. For instance, one such league of the top 50 Asian brands places some well-known names, which are regionally (and often globally) recognized as leaders in their respective sectors, at the very top of the list: Singapore Airlines, Cathay Pacific and HSBC, for example.

While we support and applaud the notion of "valuing" brands and brand strength, we believe that much work needs to be done to create a more robust system of measurement for such tables. Their key limitation is that they ignore many "local" brands and particularly the strength of brands in relation to "bonded" customers, as discussed in Chapter 6.

Of course, some local brands are included: the Shangri-la Hotel chain which includes some of the best hotels in the world; Lee Kum Kee from Hong Kong, one of the oldest brands in Asia and one which dominates the Chinese oyster sauce market in 40 countries around the world; Acer (now also known as BenQ) the global computer company from Taiwan; and Star TV which, although owned by Rupert Murdoch, is the first Asian satellite TV provider and now reaches 300 million viewers in 53 countries across Asia and the Middle East.

However, these are the exceptions, not the rule, and this type of league table merely reinforces the established view of Asia as seen through the "trading" lens of Hong Kong and Singapore in particular. It is notable that Soundblaster, a "brand" of PC soundcard founded only a few years ago in Singapore, ranks number seven on the list, and that 27 of the top 50 names come from Hong Kong and Singapore. Assessing brand strength by certain traditional criteria such as geographic spread (a major factor in the survey) creates a false picture, because with a relatively small home market, brands from Hong Kong and Singapore have to export to survive.

Korea, with a strong list of household names such as Samsung, LG and Hyundai, had no brand in the table, and China only one — TsingTao beer. Japan is not included in the survey and the size and scale of that market probably deserves a completely separate study.

Quantifying brand strength

An alternative approach, and probably more informative, is to measure what lies behind the making of a strong brand and make a full and fair assessment of all the brand "equities".

And we can do this quantitatively, by looking at how local brands have successfully generated a loyal brand relationship with their consumer franchise. The WPP research database BrandZ allows us to evaluate exactly this, and can give us an accurate measure of how well consumers have bonded with a particular brand.

As we have seen in Chapter 6, a so-called "Bonded" consumer is one who has an emotional or rational connection with a brand, to the extent that they lavish the majority of their category spend on that brand. In other words, these are the highly valuable, loyal customers who repeatedly buy your brand — definitely the right kind of customers to have.

In Japan, seven of the top 10 brands with the highest level of Bonded consumers on the BrandZ database are local Japanese brands. In Taiwan, and likewise in India, five out of the top 10 are local brands. Not bad at all. But in China, local brands account for just three of the top 10. So far, it would seem, the multinationals have been getting it right.

One good example of this comes from P&G, and its shampoo brand developed for the local market in China — Rejoice. The BrandZ data shows that an incredible 31% of consumers have Bonded with this brand — something that is only matched by more emotive brands such as Coke and Nike. No other brand in the hair-care category even comes close to that level of loyalty.

Another good example is Colgate. Having invested in building a trustworthy and respected brand by carefully building knowledge about the protective qualities of its toothpaste, Colgate has been rewarded with a fiercely loyal base of "Bonded" consumers: 34% of respondents choose Colgate time and time again.

So it would appear that we have a situation where local brands are succeeding in creating awareness, while the multinationals are succeeding in creating loyalty.

Key axes of success

The dynamics that divide local and multinational companies can be boiled down to three main axes:

1. **Culture**

   A truly local company has a commercial instinct attuned to the market and the consumer. They can be lightening-quick to market, can respond rapidly to changes, and, most importantly, are not afraid to experiment with new formulations and different marketing techniques. Multinationals, on the other hand, are more hampered by rigid procedures — time-hungry research, a corporate culture which discourages entrepreneurial adroitness, long decision-making lines, and an inherent culture of caution.

2. **Finances**

   Multinationals tend to have deeper pockets, and are less susceptible to currency fluctuations. They have a history of investing their way out of trouble, and can shift funds between markets to achieve their goals. Local companies, even those active in several markets across Asia, cannot bring the heavy-duty financial guns to bear on their competition. They need to rely on local popularity to see them through.

3. **Distribution**

   Local companies have a far more practical and "familiar" approach to securing distribution. Multinationals are hampered by being "outsiders" and control is very difficult to attain. Multinationals fear (quite rightly) that unless they own the distribution system, they will be edged out completely.

It would seem that the obvious strategy for multinational companies is to concentrate on making their brands as "local" as possible. And this is, in fact, exactly what we find happening.

Outsiders vs insiders

The result of this increased focus on "glocalization" is that once a market has lived with a variety of "multinational" brands for a while, those brands cease to be "outsiders", and start to become "one of ours". Time and time again, when asked, consumers fail to distinguish between multinational and local brands. Sunsilk is Thailand's number-one shampoo — and is considered a local brand. The same holds true for Milo in Malaysia and Volkswagen in Shanghai.

This is hardly surprising when, in many of these countries, the multinational companies are both manufacturing and selling the brands *locally*. Furthermore, global companies are often the owners of so-called local brands — how "local" is Thums Up in India, when every purchase of this iconic "local" cola brand generates revenue for the world's largest global brand company?

Similarly, Unilever owns and manages scores of "local" brands, from teas to detergents, which compete with their global brands. A classic example is Molto in Indonesia. It was for a long time a hugely successful brand of fabric softener, started and run by a local man and about six staff. Seeing the opportunity to compete head-on with another successful local brand, So-Klin, run by a Surabayan corporation called Wings, Unilever stepped in and bought Molto. As a consumer, would you distinguish between these two as multinational or local? Presumably not.

Across Asia, there is no clear division of provenance amongst consumers — they do not see a Unilever brand as Dutch or British or multinational — they are simply all "local" to the extent that they are all *"available here"* (in fact, Unilever has been in Indonesia for over 100 years — many of the so-called "local" brands are just recent upstarts in comparison). Unless a brand makes specific reference to its foreign provenance to create an advantage, it is hard to distinguish the brands on the shelf by origin. Even marketing sophistication is no longer a dividing issue. Any company, both local and multinational, has access to the best and brightest marketing minds through the global Agency network.

Strong vs. weak brands

We would suggest, therefore, that it is no longer meaningful to talk about local and multinational brands. While it is possible to distinguish between multinational and local *companies*, the real debate for the next decade (and beyond) will be about strong and weak *brands*.

To whom does the future belong?

Strong brands are invariably 360 Degree brands — the evidence from around the world is overwhelming. Brands which simply rely on mono-media communications strategies, that fail to engage the consumer at any contact point other than the main media channels, that divorce brand marketing from business strategy or packaging design or customer service — these brands can only be weak in comparison to what a truly 360 Degree brand can achieve.

The future belongs to strong, 360 Degree brands that are built around big ideas. It may matter less who owns that brand (although there is evidence of the corporate brand being used to endorse product brand communication in many markets), where it comes from, whether it is local or regional or international, if it is an established brand or a challenger, if it targets old consumers or young ones; any brand, *and any business*, will be enhanced and strengthened by developing a more inclusive, *integrated* attitude to brand development.

Anything less and the brand, the business and the client are being short-changed. Therefore, we believe that all "brand practitioners" here in Asia have an *obligation* to permeate their agencies, their client's business and the brands that are in their care with fully integrated, commercially minded 360 Degree brand thinking.

Looking at brands in this way does require a fundamental shift in perspective which can, for some, be uncomfortable. A certain level of resistance to 360 Degree brand thinking is inevitable — from those who are happy and comfortable "doing it the way it has always been done". But the world is changing rapidly, the brand landscape moves on perpetually, and the financial argument for putting the brand at the center of everything a business does is now too compelling for these nay-sayers to ignore.

But we are really still only at the beginning of the process. Even here in Asia, a region which has embraced a strong attitude towards 360 Degree Branding®, this type of brand communications approach is still in its infancy. There is still lots to be done.

The Challenge

In the spirit of 360 Degree brand development, it seems appropriate to finish this book by offering you, the reader, a brief of sorts — specifically, a 360 Degree Brand-Builder's Challenge. If our *objective* is to develop strong, world-class 360 Degree brands here in Asia that can provide the propulsion for a Pacific Century, what then, is the key challenge we all need to address in order to achieve that?

As we know from Chapter 4, the Challenge will be obvious once we have worked out what the Block is. So, what is the one thing that is preventing a greater and wider adoption of 360 Degree brand thinking?

What's the Block?

Many Asian businesses still largely operate in a manner that reflects Asia's trading heritage. Compared to service-led economies such as the U.K. and U.S., Asia is still trade-dominated. As a proportion of all business, trading in Asia still retains a huge share. Its roots go back to colonial times and before. Trading is a profitable and noble enterprise, but it creates what we might call a "selling environment" and a culture that is sales/margin orientated. This is very different to a marketing environment.

This marketing environment is still under-developed in Asia. And until you build a marketing culture, it will be difficult to implement 360 Degree brand thinking that truly permeates a corporation's culture and operations.

The road to 360 Degree implementation

There might be said to be four stages to full 360 Degree brand implementation.

- <u>Step One</u> involves a company embracing the concept of "brand" and "marketing" in general, and using straightforward conventional channels to "advertise" this brand.
- <u>Step Two</u> might represent the development of a brand's marketing output into a more dynamic and integrated communications program, involving a coordinated use of (for example) public relations, sales promotions, point-of-purchase, e-commerce and web presence, as well as advertising.
- <u>Step Three</u> represents the stage where the brand becomes internalized within a corporate culture; when the brand message is aimed at a company's own employees, in order to give the people who make, craft and sell that brand a clear set of values to work by. This ensures that the brand (and its values and personality) are represented properly at every contact point the company has with all of its customers and stakeholders.
- <u>Step Four</u> occurs when the brand begins to influence the entire suite of corporate operations, from new product development to training, from the design of the uniforms to

supply chain management. Here a brand could be said to have achieved 360 Degree "enlightenment".

As we have already discussed, by 2003, many (if not most) brand companies in Asia will have reached Step One. And as we can see from many of the case studies in this book, there are countless examples of how brands here in Asia have also embraced Step Two.

There is, however, a way to go before we will see a wholesale Step Three internalization of the brand. To put this into some sort of perspective, here is a quotation from the WPP Annual Report — 2001.

> *"The importance of internal communications has grown steeply over the past few years. Making sure that internal audiences are onside is critically important in ensuring strategic and structural messages are transmitted to customers, clients, suppliers, investors, journalists, analysts, governments and non-governmental organizations."*

There is currently less internalization of the brand here in Asia. However, believe that this will change, and that it represents one of the larger opportunities for our industry as a whole here in this region.

Consequently, there are also few examples of brands here in Asia that have developed to the point where the brand strategy begins to influence the corporate strategy (Step Four), where a full understanding of brand equity is a precondition for new product development or staff training, for example. To be truthful, there are but few examples of this in any region.

The Challenge facing Asian brand stewards

By understanding this four-step development, we can see that there is still plenty of scope for work. And we can also see how and why Asian brands and businesses can change to profit from this, and what obstacles might need to be overcome to achieve full 360 Degree Branding®.

Hence, this would suggest that the Challenge for us all is to continue to convince clients, brand owners and decision-makers — through our words, our deeds, our case studies, and our recommendations — of the huge potential brands have to create growth, profit and shareholder value for the entire company. Or to phrase it in proper 360 Degree language:

The Objective: To develop world-class brands in Asia.

The Block: A traditional trading culture which encourages a "selling and distribution" approach, rather than a "brand and marketing" mentality.

The Challenge: Demonstrate to brand owners the unique power of 360 Degree brand communications to create both short- and long-term profit.

A 360 Degree future

It is our ardent hope that this book will go some small way towards meeting this Challenge, and that it will therefore help both Asian brands and international brands operating in Asia to deliver on the promise of the Pacific Century by making Asia the political, economic and cultural powerhouse it deserves to be.

Index

Index